Dr Hany

A Servant to the World's Poorest People

Suma Din

KUBE
PUBLISHING

Dr Hany El Banna
A Servant to the World's Poorest People

Distributed and published by
KUBE PUBLISHING LTD
Tel +44 (01530) 249230, Fax +44 (01530) 249656
E-mail: info@kubepublishing.com
Website: www.kubepublishing.com

Author Suma Din
Editor Yosef Smyth
Book/Cover design & typesetting Shakir Cadir » www.opensquares.co.uk

Picture credits
The photographs in this book are used with permission and through the courtesy of:
© **Dr Hany El Banna** 13, 16 (top and bottom), 18, 19, 22 (top and bottom), 27, 83; ©
Helen Simpson p10; © **The Humanitarian Forum** 81, 85, 87, 88 (left bottom, right
bottom); © **Islamic Relief Worldwide** 28, 31, 33, 35, 37, 38, 39, 48, 52, 53, 55, 57, 58,
63, 67 (bottom), 68, 70, 72, 73, 74, 75, 77 (top and bottom), 79, 80, 92, 93 (left bottom
and right bottom); © **Istock** 12 (Paul Cowan); 14 (Luis Portugal); 21 (Ahmad Faizal); 47
(Claudio Monni); 10, 25, 39, 49, 71 (John Woodcock); © **Martijn Munneke** 67 (top)
Image on page 20 courtesy of **University of Birmingham**

The Publishers would also like to thank Islamic Relief, in particular Mohammad Afsar and
Abdul Malik, for supplying the photographs and permitting their use throughout the book.

Every effort has been made to trace and acknowledge ownership of copyright. The
Publishers offer to rectify any omissions in future editions, following notification.

A Cataloguing-in-Publication Data record for this book is available from the British Library

ISBN 978-1-8477-4026-7

Islamic Relief Worldwide and Islamic Relief Partners
have grown over a quarter of a century through the dedication of
thousands of staff, volunteers and donors. This biography, in telling
Dr Hany El Banna's story, by no means seeks to diminish the role of
all those who have given their time and effort, and in some cases their
lives, for Islamic Relief's humanitarian work.

Contents

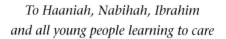

To Haaniah, Nabihah, Ibrahim
and all young people learning to care

Introduction

Dr Hany El Banna OBE is the founder of the largest Western Muslim aid and development organisation: Islamic Relief. Dr Hany's humanitarian work started in 1981 when, as a young doctor, he raised funds on the streets of Birmingham to help victims of war. His faith-driven commitment to help the poorest people in the world grew two years later when he travelled to Sudan to attend a medical conference. Witnessing the humanitarian crisis caused by a long drought Dr Hany flew into a whirlwind of activity to help.

Dr Hany in a warehouse in Zenica, Bosnia and Herzegovina

After shipping aid to Sudan, he and a colleague, Dr Ihsan Shabib, set up a committee to organise their fundraising efforts. Soon after, with more dedicated people on board, Islamic Relief (IR) – the UK's first Muslim aid organisation – was born. They set about their work in a tiny rented room with a borrowed typewriter and one phone line!

Eventually, the miniscule office became the international headquarters of Islamic Relief Worldwide (IRW), whilst IR branches sprang up in cities around the world. Over the next twenty-five years, Dr Hany and IR staff took aid and development projects wherever people were in need. Whether it was helping tsunami victims with shelter, or building a school in a remote village, IR brought hope to millions of the world's most vulnerable people. In total Dr Hany travelled to over sixty countries whilst with IR and to this day continues to work on improving the lives of whole communities with the numerous humanitarian organisations he has founded.

Born in Egypt, Dr Hany came from a scholarly and religious family. He qualified as a medical doctor and came to the UK in 1977 to continue medical research. In 1983 he returned to Cairo and married Yousreia Labib. The couple settled in Birmingham where their five children were born and raised. Today Dr Hany is the founder and president of The Humanitarian Forum, strengthening global partnerships between humanitarian charities around the world.

This story reveals the heart of a man driven by compassion and takes you into the mind of a man with fearless determination. It explains how Dr Hany deals with problems, how he sees the world and how he is motivated by his faith – Islam. Along the way he will travel up mountains, crawl through tunnels, be detained by police and cling on to grassroots – all for his mission to reach people in need!

Islamic Relief's mission is to: *'help meet the needs of vulnerable people and empower them to become self-reliant so that they can live with dignity and confidence. [They] help individuals, groups and institutions to develop safe and caring communities and make it possible for those who wish to support others to reach people in need of their help.'*

A moment back in time

'*Lebanon 1982. That was the first time I put charity work above my career.*' Dr Hany El Banna

September 1982, Dudley Road Hospital, Birmingham UK
There is a youngish-looking doctor walking home after his long shift in hospital. Slim and agile, he flies down the steps, turns the corner and crosses over the bridge at a brisk pace. His short black hair and broad eyebrows stand out against his lightly tanned complexion. Having trod this route a thousand times, he walks with familiarity.

A frown shrouds his normally playful, spirited eyes. No smile today for the kids out on the street he'd usually kick the ball to. They're disappointed but they continue their game. Just a road away from home now, he stops; a right turn would take him to the Barnes Library in the Birmingham Medical School where he should revise, straight on takes him home, where he can work out how to help. He is torn between two duties: professional exams next week to further his career or the plight of Lebanon.

He hesitates, then carries on straight.

The reports of the massacre in the refugee camps of Sabra and Shatila were hideous. The evening news showed where the carnage took place. The newspapers were worse; the details from eyewitnesses were graphic and shocking. Wars were not new to him, he had lived through three during his childhood, but what was happening in Lebanon felt different. *Right now, while I carry on with normal life there's agony, suffering and injustice meted out on innocent civilians; the women, the children, the elderly – it's horrific … What can I do?*

As his front door creaks open a bulging envelope lies on the floor. Recognising his friend's handwriting, he tears it open to find fundraising leaflets inside. He picks them up. They are to inform people about what is happening in Lebanon and to help the anguished victims. His friend must be feeling the same way. At last there is something he can do; he'll distribute these leaflets, and raise money for the victims.

The exams? His head regains control as he sits slumped over the dining table. *Four days left until the exams, but there are victims in Lebanon who need help now.* He leans back, away from the leaflets on the table.

The next morning he is at the local mosque. He approaches everyone around him, telling them about the war in Lebanon. He urges them to show compassion for the victims of the massacre and encourages them to donate what they can to help. After standing on the pavement outside the local mosque, he ventures further on to another. Encouraged with their response, he travels to a neighbouring town with the same message.

His efforts raised money, and donations were sent to The Islamic Medical Association, a charity to help the victims of war.

Three motifs of this doctor's life took root in him that week: sharing the victim's pain; communicating their suffering and need; taking action to help them. And by responding to the Sabra and Shatila massacres, it was the first time this ambitious, award-winning doctor put the condition of people suffering above his career. It was the first time Dr Hany El Banna listened to his heart.

Lebanese Civil War (1975 – 90)

This civil war started in June 1975 as a result of tensions between different factions inside and outside of Lebanon. It started in South Lebanon and affected Beirut, the capital. The war involved armies from Israel, Syria and Lebanon. Thousands of soldiers and civilians died during the war.

The Sabra and Shatila Massacres

Sabra and Shatila are two long term refugee camps in Beirut, Lebanon. Together they house thousands of Palestinian civilians in an area less than one square mile in size. On 16 – 18 September 1982, civilians were attacked by one of the warring factions in the Lebanese Civil War. Men, women and children's mutilated bodies were found strewn all over the streets of this camp on the third day, when journalists entered to report the atrocity to the world's press.

CHAPTER 1

Made in Egypt

'A father gives a child nothing better than a good education.' The Prophet Muhammad

December 1950, Cairo

Hany Abdel Gawad El Banna was born on December 9th 1950 in his grandmother's house. Her home was situated in the old part of Cairo, where historic landmarks were never far away. For Hany, growing up in the old part of Cairo brought him close to the history of Egypt, and its beautiful architecture; the lyrical minarets and domes from which the call to prayer resounded; and to the ornate arches, and the engraved columns and pillars. All of which connected him to the cultural and religious legacy of the city.

Hany was the youngest of four children to Sheikh Abdel Gawad El Banna and Nafisa Al-Jerisi. Sheikh El Banna was a magnanimous man, confident and approachable. He upheld the long family custom of graduating from the prestigious Al Azhar University, where he left as a respected sheikh (religious teacher) and a professor of Islamic Law. He was nicknamed *'the man of yellow books'* as in his possession were numerous old volumes of religious and legal texts.

Hany's mother was a learned lady who loved to read classic and contemporary books. She invested her energy in raising her children and managing all of the social connections of extended family and friends. Hany recalls his mother was a *'natural born leader'*; one whom he respected and obeyed, especially if he wanted to avoid her displeasure.

Al Azhar University

Al Azhar University, linked to the Al Azhar mosque, was originally founded as a madrasa, or centre for religious learning, in the 10th century CE. It reached international significance as one of the world's foremost centres for students to study Arabic, *sharia* (Islamic law) and the Qur'an. Al Azhar produced many famous scholars who taught around the world. In the 1950's the curriculum was expanded to include more faculties such as medicine, astronomy, geography and history, and was then formally recognised as a university.

Growing up in 'the house of the nation'

Beyond vocation and books, both Hany's parents made the Islamic faith the bedrock of their home, nurturing their children with Qur'anic values: respecting family, taking responsibility for those less fortunate than themselves and valuing education. Both parents imparted knowledge about Prophets from the past and the importance to learn from their examples. Most importantly they, as parents, modelled the values they taught their family.

Hany's father nicknamed their home *'the house of the nation'* because it was open to all who came there, whether they were neighbours or relatives. Most evenings the living room doubled as a neighbourhood court as his parents would listen to complaints and conflicts, solving disputes and making peace. Some people came with financial problems, others with marital issues. One thing was consistent throughout, all of them were seen and helped. Hany grew up in this live theatre, watching the dramas of daily life, witnessing how fact could be stranger than fiction. At the same time he experienced compassion in action. Caring for people wasn't a vague idea, a distant virtue of saintly people, it was a tangible reality, and something he heard and saw every day. In particular, Hany's mother was exemplary in how she listened to the voice of the vulnerable and the way she responded.

Hany's parents Sheikh El Banna and Nafisa Al-Jerisi

Childhood and education

Hany attended primary and secondary schools in Cairo, close to the family's house. Under his mother's watchful eyes, he and his siblings were expected to do their best in their school studies. But come the weekly holiday on Friday, friends would visit and together they watched films, played football or games with children from the neighbourhood.

From the age of nine, Hany showed an appetite for exploring and independence. His parents observed this and they debated the suitability of one particular request. One summer, when he was ten, Hany and some neighbourhood friends decided they wanted to explore Cairo's Citadel. Built by Salah ad-Din in the 12th century, the famed fortress occupied a vantage point from where the whole of Cairo could be seen. What an adventure for young Hany and his friends: they could pretend they were soldiers, mounting the fort to spot the enemy afar. Or they

could go to the military museum to see real fighter jets that were on display. After careful consideration, his parents allowed him to walk the half-hour route to the Citadel, as long as he promised to be back before evening.

His successful trip to the Cairo Citadel earned his parent's trust, and whet his appetite to go further afield. Soon after, Hany found out there was a day trip organised by older boys in the neighbourhood to visit the Japanese Gardens, twenty-five kilometres away from central Cairo, in a suburb called Helwan. Keen to explore again, he begged to join them on their trip even though it meant catching a train from Cairo out to Helwan. Family discussions ensued and after giving it much thought, he was given the permission to travel with the older boys. The Japanese Garden took Hany into a world of Buddhist statues, pagodas and ornately carved wooden bridges stretching over canals. He revelled in the freedom to explore the heritage of another civilisation. The confidence he gained to travel long distances at a young age would be a necessity in the future.

Locally, sometimes Hany wandered off to visit the school where his father was the head teacher. In the school grounds was a vineyard, date palms, shrubs and plants. While he roamed the gardens one day, he saw ripe, mouth-watering grapes hanging and was about to pick some. Hany's father soon stopped him as the grounds were the property of the school therefore a teacher's child had no right to eat the fruit. Growing up under his father's meticulous standards, Hany's sense of right and wrong was sharpened at every opportunity.

Hany aged six years

Halfway through his secondary school education, Hany's father accepted a teaching post at the Islamic University in Benghazi, Libya. His father thought it would be a good opportunity for his son, now in his teens, to travel with him and study in a secondary school nearby with an impressive library. It was here, in Benghazi, between the ages of 15 and 17 years that Hany discovered the writings of some leading voices in literature. Among them was Hany's favourite, Tawfiq

When I was young ...

... I was spoilt and mischievous in primary school. One year we had a timid and simple Arabic teacher and my friends and I often gave him trouble, teasing him. I grew out of it when I got older, but I could be mean at the time.

Al-Hakim, an attorney by profession, turned playwright. His novels moved him with their personal style, a method of communication he sought to use in his life. Other popular fiction such as Sherlock Holmes intrigued Hany, as the detective genre kept him captivated.

After gaining his secondary school certificates, Hany returned to

Cairo and successfully gained a place at Al Azhar University. It was Hany's mother's dream that at least one of her children would become a doctor. As the youngest, and last to go to university, all eyes were set upon him to fulfil his mother's wishes and he obliged. His three elder siblings studied business and the arts.

Whilst Hany's medical studies occupied most of his time, he still found ways to be an active volunteer at Al Azhar. One of his lecturers

set up a Friendship Group to organise trips and activities for undergraduates. Hany took part and put his inquisitive nature to use and organised excursions to South Egypt to visit the historic sites of Luxor and Aswan. Halfway through his course, in 1973, Egypt was involved in a conflict in the Middle East. To help, the Friendship Group set up a First Aid training programme which Hany, and the other members, delivered in local secondary schools in Cairo. The war of '73 also inspired Hany to write a play. One of the girls' secondary

Hany aged 16 years

schools he was acquainted with allowed Hany to organise a production of it, bringing his poetry into the public arena for the first time, but not the last. Hany's time in Al Azhar was thus varied and rich in experiences.

As his medical studies drew close to the end, there was one more thing he wanted to do: a diploma in Islamic Studies. This completed Hany's studies at Al Azhar University, and by 1976, the young, newly qualified doctor was ready for his first job.

Hany as a medical student in Cairo

CHAPTER 2

Laying roots in the UK

'Whoever has consciousness of God, He will make matters easy for him.' The Qur'an; chapter 65, verse 4

Qualifying as a doctor marked a family milestone as well as a personal achievement for Dr Hany. The time had now come for him to start professional life. He had two choices in front of him; an excellent position in a hospital in Jeddah, Saudi Arabia, or as his parent's preferred, the option to further his medical studies and work in the UK.

Dr Hany's parents were ambitious, and recognised their son was capable of excelling further in the field of medicine. After making enquiries about work and study in the UK Hany was offered work in the National Health Service (NHS). What faced him was at once an exciting opportunity and a daunting prospect. *'I was in tears on the plane. The reality of leaving all my family, starting a new life of work away from everyone was a tough decision to make.'*

With a heavy heart, Hany landed in London in 1977. Nothing could have prepared him for the utter contrast in climate and culture he encountered. After a brief stay in London, he travelled to Aberystwyth in

Wales to start training in a hospital. Trying to find his feet, Dr Hany had to overcome many hurdles. All at once it felt as though there were problems in every direction; financially, though he had his parent's support, living in the UK was very expensive in comparison to Cairo; he'd failed his English language exam and he was lonely and desperately missing his family. And of all the adjustments Hany had made, the weather still had the power to make him homesick.

For the next year, Dr Hany crisscrossed the UK, training in hospitals and sitting more exams to qualify him as a junior doctor. Eventually, he got his first job as a locum in a hospital in Reading, working in radiotherapy and medical oncology. A year later, he was working in a hospital in Glasgow.

Working in Glasgow in 1979

Over time, Dr Hany became too occupied by his work in the ENT (Ear, Nose and Throat) department, to notice his environment. He was often working an eighteen-hour day, with night shifts and weekend rota too. But this soon came to a natural end when he saw an advert in the BMJ (British Medical Journal), advertising a position in Dudley Road Hospital in Birmingham. A position he earnestly wanted. He was delighted when he got this post as it gave him more control over the hours he worked and he liked Birmingham, where he already had friends.

Some of Hany's friends at the time were involved in raising funds in response to international crises, and living amongst them allowed Hany to join their efforts when he could. In addition, many of them were involved in the Federation of Students Islamic Societies (FOSIS), which had its headquarters in London. Hany was part of the committee, taking on various offices of responsibility.

Hany continued work in Birmingham, as he branched out to combine clinical work as well as research in Birmingham University's Medical School. His aptitude and skill earned him the Hamilton Bailey prize for research in 1981 – the result of diligent investigation about the diagnosis of stomach cancer. At the same time, he had professional exams looming, to gain membership to the Royal College of Pathologists. With the little time he could spare after his hospital shifts, he was in the Barnes Library studying and preparing. Three days before the exams, news about the war in Lebanon and the massacres at the Sabra and Shatila refugee camps were in the headlines. A surge of responsibility awoke in Hany, and he felt compelled to help the victims that very weekend in September before his exams. By coordinating with student friends from London, and following his heart, he set out that weekend to raise funds, but by doing so failed the exam the following week.

Dudley Road Hospital residence 1982

The fleeting pilgrimage

In spite of the exam setback, working and studying in Birmingham had so far been a fulfilling experience. However, by the end of 1982, Dr Hany's contract with Dudley Road hospital was coming to an end, and he faced two choices. He could either accept a better-paid job in a hospital in Manchester, or stay on in Birmingham, in a research post at a modest income. Dr Hany had grown to like Birmingham and this city was the first place that felt like home after he had left Cairo. On the other hand, the Manchester job offer was attractive and would mean a certain move up the career ladder.

By the end of the week he still hadn't made a decision. Another day faded away and it was time to offer the night prayer known as *Isha*. At the end of the prayer, Hany sat engulfed in stillness, feeling as though he was in the presence of God, The Guide. He made a personal prayer – a plea for guidance; '*What does God want for me? What is best for my future?*' It wasn't long before he fell asleep, confident, peaceful and sure he would be guided. He began to dream.

Dressed as a pilgrim on Hajj (the pilgrimage to Makkah, Arabia) he was walking around a cube-shaped building. Was it the Ka'ba, at the centre of the great mosque in Makkah? Hany was enveloped with a tranquil feeling. All feelings of uncertainty had vanished. He walked the seven circuits around the building, engrossed in prayer. But something was out of place. The grey brick building with four floors looked familiar to him as he walked around it. He was puzzled: surely the Ka'ba did not have four floors.

By the time he woke up, he realised that in his dream he was walking around the Barnes Library in the Medical School of Birmingham University. It wasn't the Ka'ba after all, even though he was on a pilgrimage in his dream. For Hany, his prayers that night had been answered. He felt secure in his choice.

'I believed God didn't want me to take the job in Manchester.
He wanted something different for me – something that required
me to stay in Birmingham
and carry on with the
research job. Working or
worshiping or both, I had
to stay put.'

Medical faculty Univercity of Birmingham

Makkah and the Ka'ba

Makkah, in Saudia Arabia, is the holiest city for Muslims in the world. It is where the grand mosque (masjid al haram) is situated.

The **Ka'ba** is in the centre of the grand mosque and is a cube-shaped building. Muslims believe this to be the place of worship from the time of Prophet Abraham. When Muslims visit this mosque in Makkah, part of the act of worship is to walk around the Ka'ba seven times while reciting prayers.

Marriage

In the following year, 1983, getting married was on Dr Hany's mind. Seven years of bachelor life was unusual for a man from his family. The traditional stepping stones – student life, profession, marriage, and his own family en route to a respected position of authority – had been delayed by his dedication to his job.

As Hany's faith held a central place in his family's life, he wanted to marry a woman who shared the same Islamic beliefs as his family. Moreover, in the past seven years, Hany had time to research Islam beyond what he learnt in Cairo and it was an invaluable part of his life. He spent time reading books and attending talks in mosques in different cities. He was also aware, for example, that according to traditional Muslim texts, a person is advised to marry someone who is conscious of God in all that they do, putting faith before beauty, wealth or social status.

In Egyptian culture, like other Eastern cultures, it's traditional for the parents to find suitable partners for their sons and daughters. So it was a natural step for Hany to tell his parents he would like to get married, in the hope they would find or suggest a prospective match. On a telephone conversation one day, he shared his thoughts and the news that he'd be visiting Cairo for a holiday in the near future. When Hany left Birmingham, he was contemplative about the future.

Dr Hany's mother was pleased to know her son was now ready to get married. A spiritual and religious lady by nature, she took nothing for granted. Ten years ago she had dreamt that a very close family friend had given her the most exotic, sought-after fruit in Cairo in the 1970's – an apple. She took this dream to be a good sign between the families. Maybe her eldest son would one day marry a daughter from this family they had known for decades. Nothing was in her hands she resolved at the time; she put her trust in God and hoped something good may happen. A decade passed, her eldest son married someone else and like an old photograph, her dream of receiving the precious apple faded.

Above: Dr Hany with a friend
Below: Dr Hany in Bristol

When he arrived in Cairo, there was a social gathering at a family friend's house. There, that evening, one young lady's reserved, unassuming manner caught Hany's attention. From a distance she seemed good-natured. There was an uncomplicated, yet quietly confident air about her. When he met her, he thought to himself: '*She is the one.*'

In contrast, Hany, the doctor from England, was an extrovert by nature and had all the right qualities, the young lady, Yousreia was looking for. He was intelligent, quick-witted and ambitious.

Dr Hany discussed the idea of marrying her with his parents. His mother was delighted with the match. Yousreia's father was the family friend she dreamt of all those years ago, and the precious gift he gave her, the apple, now made sense to her: Hany would marry his daughter. Her dream would come true!

As the parents knew each other well, the wedding was easy to organise and could take place before Hany had to return to England. Ten days after they met they were married in the large garden of Yousreia's family home, surrounded by friends and relatives. Hany had to return to work in England immediately after, and within two months, his wife joined him to start their married life together. Hany was confident that the two prayers he made that year had been answered; he was settled in Birmingham in his job, and he felt blessed to be married to a person who shared the same conviction in faith.

Yousreia Labib

Yousreia Labib was born in Cairo to a family of Turkish and Egyptian heritage. One of six sisters and one brother, Yousreia grew up in a stately house, with extended family and a very sociable atmosphere. Her maternal side of the family was well known for the generations of Mayors they produced, who served South Cairo's civil population. Yousreia graduated in business and administration at Cairo University before marrying Dr Hany and moving to the UK.

CHAPTER 3

Finding a vision in Sudan

'The best of you is he (or she) who is of most benefit to others.' The Prophet Muhammad

While Dr Hany worked at Dudley Road Hospital, and continued to study at the medical school in Birmingham University, reports of a devastating famine in Sudan were headline news. Like many people at the time, he was shocked and dismayed at what he saw. He discussed the situation with friends and brainstormed ideas at a FOSIS committee meeting to help the victims of the famine. The committee voted for him to go on a trip there, to a medical conference, and see the situation for himself. Dr Hany knew Khartoum, the capital of Sudan, fairly well as he had travelled there in his teens with his father.

There was one obstacle; he couldn't afford the ticket to get there. Instead of giving up the plan, he approached an old friend of his father, the Imam of Regent's Park Mosque, for help. The Imam was keen to help the young doctor, and lent him the money so he could make his way to Sudan.

Famine in the Horn of Africa

The Horn of Africa is the north-east region of the African continent. It is made up of seven countries; Eritrea, Djibouti, Ethiopia, Somalia, Kenya, Uganda and Sudan. Over the past century, this area has been affected by conflicts over ethnicity, religion and territory. In addition drought, famine and widespread disease have afflicted this region.

In 1983, one of the worst famines in the region occurred. The famine was caused by a combination of factors such as drought and civil war. Various ethnic groups and political factions from North and South Sudan were embroiled in a civil war which resulted in an economic crisis that the Government did not address. The drought caused agricultural problems resulting in huge food shortages. In addition wars between Eritrea and Ethiopia resulted in an increase in refugees who came to Sudan looking for help. Television images and newspaper reports shocked the world's viewers with the images of thousands upon thousands of humans starving.

In December 1983 he set off for Sudan, in the company of other doctors. When Dr Hany touched down in the capital of Khartoum, he asked the taxi driver to take him to all of the five-star hotels in the city – he was sure he would find the conference at one of them. After a frantic search, they eventually reached the Grant Hotel at 3am, where the conference was being held.

After attending the conference he was eager to see the reality for the local citizens and asked to visit refugee camps. He was dumbstruck by the conditions. Instant shock. Orphaned infants waited to die under trees – lacking the energy to call out for their parents. Men and women were too weak to look for food, their bodies exposing their skeletons. Some people leant against the walls of a medical centre expressionless, awaiting death to end their suffering. Among the hundreds of thousands dying from malnutrition were refugees from Eritrea who had left their villages in search for food. The dusty dry climate, high temperatures, and lack of sanitation made disease spread all the more quickly. Dr Hany was reviled by the conditions he saw in the refugee camps. It was particularly painful to witness the scarcity of resources, when he knew the rest of the world had enough to help them.

A year earlier, Dr Hany propelled himself into action to help the victims of the Lebanese civil war. This experience in Sudan stirred all that he had felt in 1982. As the plane took off, he left behind the human misery of Khartoum, but he held onto the images of those faces he had seen without hope. He didn't need to think over the best course of action, or evaluate what he could do about the situation. What he experienced gripped his heart and all he could hear was one man, possessing just enough strength to speak, pleading *'For God's sake, do something for us'*. On the flight from Khartoum, scenes from Sudan flicked through Hany's mind like a motion picture: the look of desperation in the eyes of the mother cradling her dying child; the hopeless gaze in the sullen faces of the elderly suffering silently, the whimpers of children – scene after scene played back to him. He knew what he needed to do once he was back in England, but first, with a short stop in Cairo planned, he'd make a start.

The first donation

As soon as he arrived in Cairo, he showed pictures of Sudan to his family, relating what he had seen to them in the hope he would raise funds. Sat amongst Dr Hany's brothers and sisters was a young nephew called Bassem. He listened intently as his uncle recounted, in graphic detail, what the famine was causing. Bassem had the equivalent of 20p in his pocket, money he had saved for a chocolate bar. When his uncle finished speaking, he put his hand in his pocket and pulled out the coin saying: *'Take this for the people in Khartoum, I don't need the chocolate'*. That first donation encouraged Hany. He was determined to achieve the response he wanted to help the people of Sudan. Within a few days, Dr Hany left Egypt with 1500 Egyptian pounds.

Bassem, Dr Hany's nephew

Two weeks after he returned from Cairo, in mid-January 1984, Hany, a close friend Dr Ihsan Shabib, and both their families set about raising more funds for Africa. They also set up a temporary fundraising station in Birmingham's Muslim Students House on Moseley Road, where three donation boxes were placed for collections. Whenever Hany wasn't at work, he was outside the mosque – the same spot he stood raising money in 1982 – shaking a box to collect donations for the people he had witnessed dying in Africa. People coming to the mosque to perform their prayers understood the emphasis Islamic teachings placed on giving charity, however small or great. Inside the mosque, it was common to listen to the Qur'an recitation where verses such as the following were read aloud, in Arabic, to the congregation:

'God commands justice, the doing of good,
and generosity to kith and kin,
and He forbids all shameful deeds,
and injustice and rebellion.'
The Qur'an; chapter 16, verse 90

Dr Hany also travelled from town to town, echoing the pleas of the starving, the dying, and the homeless people in Africa. A family summer camp in Carlisle attended by hundreds of people gave him a platform to speak about the fundraising efforts and gain support for the fledgling organisation. There was nothing quiet about his message, it was loud and clear!

Within months Hany, Dr Ihsan and their friends and families had raised £5000. To plan how they would use the funds the circle of friends had formed a committee. Their first step was to get the help of an NGO (non-governmental organisation) working in the area to distribute their donation. After a discussion between the committee, part of it was used to build a chicken farm for Eritrean refugees in the state of Kassala, East of Sudan. The income from the farm through selling chickens and eggs would be used to provide people with shelter and food. The rest of the funds were used to buy cattle for farming and breeding livestock, and setting up education and rehabilitation projects. Dr Hany made another

trip to East Sudan later in the year to visit the project sites.

IR's first project, a chicken farm in East Sudan, 1985

1984 was a landmark year; the fundraising had started to see results by supporting projects overseas and Dr Hany and his wife became parents to their first child. But this wasn't without challenges. With Hany working, studying at Birmingham University for his MD (medical doctorate), and being away from home visiting the projects, life was not easy for his wife, for whom life in the UK was still new.

However, this was just the beginning and Yousreia knew it. With another sizeable donation from a Libyan friend from Carlisle, the desire in Dr Hany had increased to do more, to help the needy in other parts of Africa where similar conditions prevailed. Just as Dr Hany and Dr Shabib intended, their work that started in Sudan in 1984 grew and multiplied like the ears of corn in the parable:

> *'The parable of those who spend their possessions for the sake of God is that of a grain out of which grow seven ears, in every ear a hundred grains: for God grants manifold increase unto whom He wills; and God is Infinite, All–Knowing.'*
>
> The Qur'an; chapter 2, verse 261

CHAPTER 4

Realising relief

'By no means will you gain righteousness until you give freely of what you love.' The Qur'an; chapter 3, verse 92

Dr Hany and the newly formed committee were soon into their second year of fundraising and they needed a name, a banner under which they could start an organisation. A singer and song-writer called Yusuf Islam (formerly known as Cat Stevens) who was equally moved by the conditions in Africa, suggested 'Islamic Relief'. That seemed a good idea, the group agreed.

'Islamic' reflected the values from the Qur'an: *'Whoever saves a life of one human being, it is as though they have saved the life of humanity'.* While 'Relief' summed up the charity's aim: *'To relieve people from their suffering.'*

In the same year, 1985, Islamic Relief's (IR) first two bank accounts were opened to receive donations; one for general donations, the second for Zakat donations, a tax that any adult Muslim with sufficient means has to pay. With this in place Dr Hany set his sights high; sending relief was not all he wanted to achieve. He wanted to make long-term improvements for the drought victims in Sudan. This meant Islamic Relief would need to set up a field office in Khartoum. Its function would be to create long-term projects for housing, education, and healthcare, and to help people get jobs. The aim was to see the population of Sudan start 'living' and stop 'surviving'.

Setting up the office in Sudan was very difficult. Dr Hany remembers how, *'There were many challenges, no roads between villages, no organised way of doing things. We had to charter planes to get to places we wanted to reach.'*

Over the next year, the Sudanese people suffered even more. A ravishing flood and the ongoing civil war demanded the young new group step up its efforts to raise funds. And they rose to the challenge. That year, Dr Hany and a group of volunteers stood outside Regent's Park mosque in London to collect donations after the Eid Prayer. In that one morning, they mobilised the congregation to raise £1500 – a huge amount in 1986 and just the type of success they needed to motivate them to aim higher and push harder.

Zakat

Zakat is one of the five pillars of Islam, a set of obligations on each Muslim. Any Muslim, who has some wealth left after their basic needs are met, must donate at least two per cent of it every year towards helping the poor and needy. Zakat is used in a variety of ways including: educating children, providing food and housing to the needy and organising social welfare projects.

First Home

By 1985, with Islamic Relief established, their bank account open for donations and an energetic team involved, their 'office' needed extending. Dr Hany and the rest of the committee went from having three donation boxes on the wall to sharing a space with another organisation and having two cabinets, a phone line and an answering machine. By 1986 they had moved again. This time they had a space of their own, which was equivalent to the size of a cupboard, measuring three meters by three meters. This became IR's headquarters. In addition to the phone line they hired a telex-machine and a supporter donated an historic '286' model computer. Some second hand furniture and a borrowed typewriter gave the semblance of a place of work.

During the day, Dr Hany paced hospital corridors in his white coat; during the evening he worked on the projects to help people in Africa. Piles of post would greet him when he visited the office. Dr Hany would sit at the solitary desk and begin to sift through the mail. Envelope after envelope would be carefully opened, in the hope of collecting more cheques from donors. Some people wrote in with queries, others communicated their willingness to volunteer and help the new organisation. Some letters revealed the difficulties of people in tough circumstances in the UK, who asked the charity for help.

I don't ask how?

When I get an idea, a vision of what I want to achieve, I don't get stuck at 'how' I'm going to do it. I just go for it! That's my philosophy: if you're in a dark tunnel – keep walking, you'll get to the end, you'll reach the light. I put my trust in God and keep working and things work out.

Tuesday evenings and Saturday mornings were the regular times medical students, who volunteered for the charity, would come into the office to organise the paperwork. At any given evening or weekend, there were multiple ideas and projects to work on. For instance they were organising a huge clothes collection and trucks were needed to send it all to Guinea, Mozambique and Ghana. Other projects they were organising were the shipment of 300 000 tonnes of wheat to Mozambique, and setting up a mobile health clinic for orphans in Pakistan.

Dr Hany and the team had also decided to make a short documentary and a photo exhibition to publicise the need to send aid to people in the Horn of Africa. If people weren't aware of the problems people faced, why would they give aid?

Raising Awareness

Dr Hany's strategy to raise awareness was two-fold. Firstly, he wanted Muslims to understand the humanitarian teachings in the Qur'an about giving charity, feeding and sheltering the displaced, and relieving someone's suffering, in the hope this would mobilise them to help in whatever way they could. The second part of the strategy was to raise awareness that Islamic Relief could help Muslims fulfil their humanitarian obligations. By doing this he was constructing the plan for Islamic Relief to flourish. He visualised the architecture before the volunteers and committee members filled in the bricks and mortar. As the spokesperson his message was clear, and it gave the volunteers confidence and clarity in the organisation's faithful direction.

In addition to a message, Islamic Relief needed a logo so its swelling rank of supporters could recognise it. A Turkish artist volunteered to design one to symbolise Islamic Relief's message. The logo fit the vision the founders had and was soon to be seen on all the material Islamic Relief was rapidly producing to publicise their campaigns. Stickers, posters, leaflets and prayer cards with Islamic Relief's details on it entered Muslim households throughout the UK.

Making Islamic Relief a household name was only achieved through the determination of the families that worked alongside Hany. Dr Shabib's wife, known as Umm Nur (Arabic for 'Nur's mother'), ran a ladies study group. She and Yousreia would cook for the ladies and then fundraise for Africa. On other occasions they organised bazaars, holding them in community halls and arranging to collect donated goods from people such as clothes, toys and bric-a-brac. The funds raised from the bazaars made a direct contribution to the projects Islamic Relief began in East Sudan. In Birmingham alone, there were many other families in which parents and teenagers worked together to distribute leaflets and stickers at mosques, in schools, at shops and in local businesses. Among them was one man who translated leaflets and posters into Arabic. Further afield, the family of Tippu Sultan and Sarah Sheriff in London organised many fundraising bazaars and were responsible for raising awareness about the charity in the capital. Eventually, with the help of these families, Islamic Relief – the name, the logo and its work – was recognised in key cities across the UK.

Long-term help also came from well-off donors. In 1986, one donor lent Islamic Relief £7000 to help them with their work. Islamic Relief used this to produce 125 000 stickers and 10 000 posters with prayers from the Qur'an printed on them, and IR's logo and contact details. These were printed in Arabic, English and Urdu, and reached people across the UK, USA, Mauritius, France, and Pakistan. This initiative brought widespread support for the charity as people who read these prayers were made aware of IR's existence and started to trust and support their appeals. Furthermore the additional publicity made a massive difference, with Islamic Relief raising around £100 000 for the famine in Africa. So impressed by the success of this simple and effective project, the donor decided to make his loan a donation instead. It was support like this which contributed to IR's rapid recognition.

But as new help came, one of the pillars of the organisation was about to leave. Dr Ihsan Shabib's time as a student in the UK had come to an end and he returned to Iraq. Dr Hany missed him sorely. They had shared the same vision, and Dr Shabib's family had made sacrifices for Islamic Relief to establish itself.

'He had a smile from heaven and God blessed him with a heart of gold. He was the main support for IR in its first three years', recalled Dr Hany.

An aid truck leaving a warehouse in the mid 1980s

Practical goals

Dr Hany tried to get the message of charitable responsibility across to the younger generation too. One way he and the volunteers of Islamic Relief aimed to do this was to organise a games tournament.

The tournament was an idea sparked off in 1988 when a volunteer for IR swam 200 metres and raised £200. A few months later a volleyball tournament organised by Islamic Relief raised £1200 for Bangladesh and a 5-a-side football tournament, which had 36 teams, was initiated. Altogether, by the end of the year, 800 youths were playing in 'The Islamic Relief Games'!

With the vision of involving the community the IR Games grew. Other youth organisations worked with them and separate tournaments took place in France, Belgium and the USA. Dr Hany was pleased with the outcome: children enjoyed themselves, they learnt about poverty and the games raised funds for aid work.

Many of the teams from all over the UK would stay in Birmingham to participate in the Islamic Relief Games. During their stay, Hany would motivate them to train hard and aim to win. He also taught them prayers and inspired them with verses from the Qur'an. Among the many prayers he taught was: *'Our Sustainer, nothing is easy except what You have made easy. If You wish, You can make the difficult easy.'*

A second-year student from Wolverhampton University remembers how the volunteers coped with the IR Games experience:

> *'There was a huge organising committee for these games – about 200 volunteers coordinating for months beforehand. On the weekend of the games, we'd arrive at the NEC (National Exhibition Centre) in Birmingham, on a Friday night, laying out all the equipment for football matches, and setting the whole place up, till the early hours of Saturday morning. Teams came from the width and breadth of the UK – about five thousand participants in all. Sometimes we had to manage heated disagreements between teams – that was testing. But there was a great voluntary spirit throughout and by the end of 48 hours on our feet we would be shattered on Monday morning; I once fell asleep in a truck in the warehouse and woke up the next morning when I was supposed to be returning sports equipment to schools! But it was all worth it. IR Games was a huge milestone in the development of the organisation and included young people in the whole charitable process.'*

Jehangir Malik OBE, Islamic Relief UK Director, 2011.

In the field

'Whoever saves a life of one human being, it is as
though they have saved the life of humanity.'
The Qur'an; chapter 5, verse 32

Four years after Dr Hany's first trip
to Sudan, Islamic Relief officially
registered as a charity in 1989.
Additionally it was now renting
two rooms for the IR offices, in
the same Muslim Student House in
Mosley Road.

After dealing with the
consequences of the drought in
Africa, there was another challenge
waiting around the corner, ready
to present new tests for the staff to
overcome. Tragically, at the end of

Outside the Muslim Student House office in Moseley Road, 1991

1989 came the Khartoum flood disaster in Sudan that affected millions of refugees squatting in low-lying flood-prone areas. Responding to this required a huge amount of planning and a greater scale of fundraising. Hany and volunteers leafleted and collected donations, including a large donation from the Saudi Embassy, until they had a shipment ready to send overseas. It was the biggest they had ever organised and they were desperate to get the tents, blankets and food items to the victims. Failing to get a free airlift from the RAF (Royal Air Force) they decided to charter their own cargo plane. None of the team had any experience or knowledge of doing this yet they managed it and arrived in Sudan, ready to unload their cargo. *'Instead of being able to distribute it, we were made guests of an African Institute, uncertain of what was going to happen. In the meantime our shipment was 'held' and would not be released. We weren't prepared for the reality of a flood and how every normal system stops. Roads, buildings, communications were not functioning. We thought we'd land in Sudan and hand out aid to people standing in queues waiting for us – as easy as that! Nothing could be further from reality. This shipment was a turning point for us. We had moved on from being a two or three people effort to having a dedicated team of volunteers with real experience.'*

Unloading cargo in Sudan, 1990

In total, Islamic Relief raised a monumental £200 000 for the victims of the flood in Sudan, making it the largest relief operation in their short history. It was also a sign of the incredible progress they had made since Hany's first collection of 20p in 1983.

In 1991, Islamic Relief's immediate assistance was called upon again. It was the year of a deadly cyclone in Bangladesh. The cyclone started in the district of Chittagong, and spread to the north-east of the country claiming over a hundred thousand lives and leaving ten million people homeless. This was a devastating natural disaster, strikingly different to the famine in the Horn of Africa. Staff and volunteers worked tirelessly, often through to the early hours of the morning to produce publicity materials for fundraising. By now, Islamic Relief received national attention and their campaign was covered in BBC and ITV news bulletins, in which they urged the British public to donate so they could help the victims of the flood. Islamic Relief joined other organisations in sending medical supplies, food, water purification tablets and shelter materials to Bangladesh. All that was needed were volunteers to distribute it to the people there.

Dr Hany travelled as one of the volunteers to distribute the aid. In the capital of Bangladesh, Dhaka, the team were confronted by masses of displaced flood victims whose homes and possessions had been swept away with the cyclone, making them destitute and in much

need of the medical supplies, food packages and shelter equipment IR, as well as other aid agencies, had brought. The magnitude of the problem required the second IR field office to be set up in Bangladesh.

Field Offices

Establishing the field offices gave Islamic Relief a permanent platform to respond quickly to the needs of the community around them. From the donor's perspective, a field office was seen as a permanent commitment to supporting people in need with long-term projects, hence encouraging sponsorship.

Setting up a field office involves looking at the needs of a particular area and finding a suitable building to hire as an office. In Islamic Relief's early days, Dr Hany made several trips to the country where the office was to be set up. Whilst looking at the geographical location, road connections and other such logistics, Hany had to find suitable people to employ.

Once the office was set up, Dr Hany continued to visit them, and always insisted on sleeping in the office somewhere. This was often a side room, close to the kitchen, where he got to know workers such as the cooks and cleaners. Other times he was invited to stay in an employee's family home. For Hany this was an enriching experience where he would become part of the families that, through Islamic Relief, worked for the needy. Eventually, his experience 'in the field' helped him define the breadth and function of all Islamic Relief field offices, which focused on:

- *individual orphan sponsorship schemes supported by institutions to develop such orphans and other needy children;*
- *community training centres for the development of the community;*
- *income–generation schemes and credit loan schemes;*
- *clean water schemes;*
- *prevention of blindness schemes.*

The formula of 'crisis, communication and fund raising' Hany devised almost a decade ago remained the staple for him still. But not for him alone – the staff of approximately 20 employees worldwide, with the help of countless volunteers were forging further into the global humanitarian scene with this mantra. And after responding to the floods in Sudan and Bangladesh IR and Dr Hany had proved themselves to the world, or so they thought.

The same year, 1991, another type of challenge was brewing at home in Birmingham. The 1991 Gulf War between Iraq and Kuwait was headline news around the world. The daily air strikes, and ground attacks, gave rise to a humanitarian disaster as the number of refugees from both countries, in particular Iraq, needed support. Islamic Relief was ready to help but because of its inherent 'Islamic' associations it was intensely scrutinised to prove their funds were supporting humanitarian aid only, instead of supporting a faction involved in the war. Dr Hany, as the Managing Director, was required to defend and maintain the transparency of the charity as a global humanitarian agency. Eventually Islamic Relief succeeded as they proved all their work met international standards of an aid organisation.

After responding to the cyclone in Bangladesh and defending Islamic Relief's principles, Dr Hany had a few more goals in sight. Compelled by his faith he set out to achieve them, and in 1991 he also saw the opening of Islamic Relief branches across Europe in Scotland, Belgium, France, Germany and the Netherlands. This drive came from Hany's firm belief that he was serving God's creation, and following the example of the Prophet Muhammad. Two beliefs he had attained from many years studying Islam.

Effect of the Bangladesh flood, 1991

Soul Food

Around the time Hany started to focus on aid work, he also decided to continue his own Islamic education. To do this he set up a study circle and shared teachings about Islam. They arranged small gatherings and invited family and friends to learn with them. Many of the men and women who attended were members of the local Muslim community.

To prepare for the classes Hany read classic Muslim scholars and he reflected on the messages of the Qur'an: to work for justice, to alleviate suffering and to remove hardship from the lives of human beings. The messages emboldened Dr Hany and 'fed his soul', driving away doubts, and helping him to scale obstacles and ignore petty problems.

At every opportunity, he steered Islamic Relief with principles from the Qur'an, whether this was an overt message to the employees or simply the way he chose to handle a problem. On the other hand, Islamic Relief's code of conduct, its rules that all staff abided by, stated that humanitarian work should remain separate from the worker's faith and beliefs.

> *'Under no circumstance',* cautioned Dr Hany in an interview, *'should humanitarian work be mixed with promoting religion. Faith-based for us means translating our faith into action as our faith inspires us to help all those who are poor and vulnerable, not simply those of a particular religious denomination.'*

At home in Birmingham, life was busy for Dr Hany. In any given week he was fulfilling one of his many roles. As a student, studying for his MD (medical doctorate) at Birmingham University, he was in charge of the Egyptian Student Union. At the same time, he was an executive member of FOSIS (the Federation of Student Islamic Societies). Both these commitments demanded time, of which he had very little. Fortunately, by his side and taking the strain off his shoulders was Yousreia. She supported his deluge of commitments by managing their home and children and all that came with that role. Of this extremely busy time in his life, Dr Hany reflects, *'She made our home a haven of peace, and this played a huge part in all the work I did.'*

When I sit in a plane I...

… see the world from a new angle. Flying in among the clouds, I'm at a distance from the earth. The sky is where I start planning… the sky is not the limit, it's the beginning.

In the early days of Islamic Relief, I made several trips around Europe to set up IR offices. On one of my flights to Frankfurt I took out the world map and started planning – I drew circles around all the cities I wanted to see Islamic Relief established. Over time, these circles became offices. So the sky was the best place to plan!

CHAPTER 6

Grassroots to mountain tops

'A man is not a believer who fills his stomach while his neighbour is hungry.' The Prophet Muhammad

Dr Hany had successfully helped bring about the rapid growth of Islamic Relief. As the strategies to raise funds were so successful, more staff could be employed to plan a wider variety of projects. As a result a move to a larger office was now imminent. Larger premises were also required for the huge supplies that were collected to be sent where necessary. The small cocoon that housed Islamic Relief in Moseley Road was exchanged for the huge headquarters a road away in Rea Street. The official headquarters of Islamic Relief Worldwide was established.

Bigger headquarters meant bigger problems. Hany had to deal with more staff, which meant more personality clashes, misunderstandings and bigger teams to coordinate … all areas of potential problems. Hany's response was direct. He developed a company philosophy, setting out how a relief worker should carry out their role in an organisation serving the world's poorest. Often he would talk about this at Friday prayers during his sermons, known as *khutbas*. They were not about grand topics, rather they urged staff to reflect on their attitude, their perspective and their connection to God. He quizzed, he questioned. Blunt and to the point, he wanted each and every individual to recognise their inter-connectedness in an organisation, in a town, in the UK, and as global citizens. For Hany, speaking to his staff wasn't enough.

Comfortable with penning poems and reflections, Hany wrote a full-length manual called 'Grassroots' to guide all employees. In this he spelt out his philosophy and vision for Islamic Relief. It detailed the success and the failures of their efforts.

Rehanah Sadiq was the first female employee to work on community awareness and fundraising for Islamic Relief. Initially as a volunteer, Rehanah worked vigorously to raise funds for every relief campaign she knew about. She coordinated local women to cook for bazaars, sell home-stitched baby clothes and paint Qur'anic verses in calligraphy onto picture frames to auction. Once an employee, Rehanah had more regular contact with Dr Hany and encountered IR's philosophy first hand. She recalls:

> *'I loved working for Islamic Relief! As employees, we shared an unspoken commitment to serving God by advocating on behalf of those in need wherever they were. In those days, when you worked with someone in community work, you knew they were doing it from their heart, to please God. We were all on the same wavelength and working for the same goal, so Dr Hany's perspective felt very natural and so did his down-to-earth ways. His warm way of saying 'May Allah bless you' to us frequently gave me a sense of belonging at a time when organisations like these were few and far between.'*

Grassroots

To start with, Grassroots, Islamic Relief's company guide charted a clear message about how to relate to the communities the IR workers took aid to:

» *eat simple food with them;*
» *talk to the child and adult equally;*
» *accept invitations even from the poorest person in a community;*
» *never talk to them from a distance, as though you are from a different social class;*
» *when invited to sleep at someone's house, accept. Even if you have to sleep on the floor on a blanket, it makes their day. It is not a privilege for them if you stay with them, but a privilege for you.*

In Hany's mind there was utter clarity about the ownership of the organisation and in turn they, the employees, were required to work for them. In 'Grassroots' he asked:

'To Whom Does Islamic Relief Belong?

The owner of Islamic Relief is the poor man, the young orphans, the elderly, the needy, the lonely widows; these are the real owners of Islamic Relief. The staff of the organisation such as an officer, secretary, manager, director, trustee, chairman and others should know that they are no more than servants to the owners of the organisation.

Quite often, people get mixed up between the means and the aims. The means is the organisation and the aim is to please God through making His creation happy. We must not worship our little organisation and societies, but rather worship the One who gives us everything without needing anything from us.'

Taking action at the grassroots level was essential for Dr Hany and he suggested activities that youth groups could do:

» *voluntary rubbish collections on public holidays;*
» *environment care: planting trees with the local authority;*
» *helping the elderly: visiting old people's homes;*
» *visiting the sick in hospital;*
» *run soup kitchens for the homeless;*
» *provide social outlets for the youth through camps, games and trips.*

Grassroots in the field

As Dr Hany built the company infrastructure, which brought about growth at home in the UK, Islamic Relief also continued to grow elsehwere. After successfully working in Sudan and Bangladesh, in 1992 Islamic Relief started to work in Pakistan. With Dr Hany and IR staff making several trips to set up projects in Pakistan in the following years. On one trip he travelled to the capital of Azad Kashmir, Muzaffarabad, by road to see the water well projects Islamic Relief had arranged in remote villages.

The landscape of Azad Kashmir

As he approached Muzaffarabad he saw the striking, imposing mountains, hemming it in, with other villages nestled in between the banks and peaks. Clusters of houses and shacks were visible from the scenic mountain roads. The rugged terrain outside Muzaffarabad made the car journey difficult. Beset by breakdowns, they were often waiting for another car to arrive to continue their journey. Eventually, they arrived at the location of the 'safe-water' projects where they continued their journey on foot. Dr Hany and the local guide struggled in the heat to ascend the jagged, often slippery side of the mountain. He marvelled at the strength of the women who walked up and down the very same mountain transporting water containers on their head! When he reached the top, he saw the progress that had been made and asked the local officer when the work would be finished. When completed, the water wells would provide clean water to 54 houses, the village school, the mosque and a small market.

After descending, they took a short drive to a remote village with a government school with 350 pupils. Sat in rows on the floor in semi-darkness, with no electricity or water, Dr Hany could barely see the children. In the playground he noticed most of the children had pieces of wood to write on, whilst some had notebooks. *'They have exams'* was the reply when he enquired about the few privileged enough to have paper.

Dr Hany on Muzaffarabad's mountain top

Monday 15th September- Pallandri, Pakistan

I saw women coming back and carrying the water pots
on their heads. Again I felt as a relief worker I
am weaker than the people I am helping. I ran out
of breath by climbing half the mountain and walking
between the two distribution tanks. I really felt
like we were a group of comedians sitting on chairs
in comfortable offices and planning for people
whose suffering we cannot reach or feel. No one
can claim to be a relief worker without living the
issues of the needy.

Reflecting on a visit to a second-hand clothes warehouse in Pakistan,
he wrote:

When I entered, the smell was unbelievable. I was
going to vomit. I looked at everyone else; it all
seemed normal for them. I realised the weakness was
in me, not that they were superhuman. The relief
worker who claims that he targets and reaches the
most needy must find such smells and scenes are part
of his daily life. The smell should not offend him,
rather it should be like Jasmine [a flower].

As a result of such encounters in Pakistan Islamic Relief established a field office there in 1994.

Next on Dr Hany's schedule was a road trip to Afghanistan to assess the needs of the people in order to help them. After a 15 hour drive through the mountainous region, Hany and one local IR employee reached Kabul, the capital. On a rugged mountainside, overlooking a busy road, Hany watched mesmerised at the scene below. Blue-eyed children, with unkept light brown hair, hopped to and fro on the dangerous roads. With each quick step out onto the tarmac, they filled craters to earn a few rupees. Others lined the sides of the main road, managing their stash of used cans. As cars or walkers passed by, girls and boys no older than eight or nine years rushed towards them, thrusting the water filled used cans towards their faces in exchange for a few rupees.

Mean jeans!

I like wearing a variety of clothes: trousers, suits, jalabeya, shirwani. I prefer to wear the colour blue. I usually wear jeans on field trips, but while climbing mountains in Pakistan I found wearing a t-shirt and jeans the worst thing to wear! Heavy, hot and tight in that climate the jeans were crippling! Shalwar and kamise is much more comfortable there. One day I hope to earn the honour to wear the famous Al Azhari robe that only scholars like my father wore.

Diary Entry 17th September Muzzafarabad

I felt guilty when we were driving between
Jalalabad and Kabul because of the number of
people standing on the road asking for a lift. We
couldn't take them because of security. But have
we forgotten the saying of the Prophet Muhammad,
'Whoever among you has an extra horse or transport
to be ridden by others, he must share it.' ... our
life of comfort has made us materialistic ... The
beggar and the deprived have a right to our money.

Whichever corner of the world Hany travelled to, his diary entry
would always finish with 'lessons to learn' a personal mirror in which
nothing was spared, least of all himself. From the trips to Pakistan and
Afghanistan he concluded:

... I now understand the need of a stick to lean
on when I was going up and down the mountain.
I always claimed to be a relief worker, but I
discovered I am far away from that. ... When you
look at the man who thinks he's courageous, you
find a small mountain like this can break his back
when he tries to climb it.
    Feelings: we must feel the suffering of the
people before we try to address their needs. My
advice to everyone doing social work is to mix and be
with the people in need; to feel their suffering.

With offices throughout the world and projects underway in numerous countries the first phase of Islamic Relief was complete. Not only could they could fundraise but they had also proven they could respond to emergencies and distribute aid. Staff, volunteers and the donors, all as committed as each other, had made Islamic Relief a respected charity among people of all faiths across the world. The next move was to go beyond distributing aid and starting to establish long-term development projects. Dr Hany wanted to help the most vulnerable first: children.

Young girls in Afghanistan

CHAPTER 7

The language of love

'Smiling... is charity.' The Prophet Muhammad

Witnessing the children selling cans of water on the narrow mountain passes to Kabul highlighted the problem of child poverty worldwide. On a daily basis children were risking their lives to meet their basic needs. Some survived by their wits, for others there would be a tragic end. When Dr Hany reached Kabul, the dire reality of the lack of medical facilities

Dr Hany with refugees in Ingushetia

for children came home to him. After the trip in his hotel room in Kabul, he opened his diary:

Saturday 13th September, Kabul, Afghanistan.

Had a long tour of Kabul. The poverty is unbelievable. We went to the Children's hospital and the condition was indescribable. The hospital has 200 beds but it accommodates up to 500-600 children. The intensive care unit for post-operations and newborns has no oxygen line, it has nothing at all.

I saw a one-week-old baby who had just had an operation on the spinal cord. The baby was asleep and I could see abscesses on his face. He was being treated for infections, but I could see he would not survive.

We saw children with wounds from landmines. In the malnutrition ward we saw the severe overcrowding; two children per bed. Babies with head injuries, children in deep comas with no care … the hospital lacked everything.

We must do something. We must raise money for these projects.

Seeing children in such dire situations had a profound effect on Dr Hany. Often, to compensate for their grim circumstances he would do all he could to lift their spirits. On occasions it would work, and some children in less harsh conditions miraculously smiled, amused by the kind stranger who played with them – a fleeting visit of happiness. In countries where Arabic and English were not spoken, Dr Hany developed his own language to communicate with children in places as far apart as China and Ingushetia.

'Squawk … maaahaaa, eeeyorre! I speak 'baaahhaa' with them. Children love animal sounds and that's how I make friends. Sometimes we have laughing competitions… I laugh, then they laugh, then I laugh harder, and then they try and out laugh me. Sometimes I sing rhymes to them, even if they don't understand the words, they understand the animal sounds. One year in Juba, South Sudan I met a group of children and sang an Arab version of 'Old McDonald had a farm'. The next year when I returned, the children saw me and the first thing they did was start humming bits of the rhyme – that was what I reminded them of.'

Fuel for the heart

When you look at the child, the child inspires you. When you look at the widow, holding her baby, and her tears and her agony it fuels your heart, it ignites you to … lift the poverty and suffering.

With increasing numbers of orphaned children around the world, Islamic Relief made caring for orphans a priority. A major influence on Dr Hany to make this decision was the example of the Prophet Muhammad, who taught that a person who cares for an orphan will be next to him in Paradise.

Dr Hany with children in China

Al Yateem – the orphan

As early as 1985, Islamic Relief partnered with other orphan projects, such as one in South London. A few months later, in 1986, an IR project called 'Support an Orphan' started. Sixty orphans in Kenya were sponsored through the support of donors. The reality of how many millions of orphans there were across the globe was taken to the community. The response to this appeal was phenomenal, and more donors were soon found. Once an orphan was sponsored there were a number of ways he or she could be helped:

» *health care including vaccinations;*
» *basic necessities like food, shelter and clothing;*
» *emotional support for traumatised children;*
» *education and school equipment;*
» *vocational training in practical skills such as information technology and languages.*

The efforts of Islamic Relief's staff and the public's generosity paid off. Like many others, this idea had humble beginnings, but twenty-four years later, in 2010, there were 27 000 orphans sponsored in over twenty-two countries.

Dr Hany's warmth and kindness often stretched beyond the children and orphans he met. In the Muslim faith, nature is seen as manifestations of God's creation and power; from seeds and plants, to oceans and animals. To Dr Hany, as a Muslim, it meant he felt a sense of responsibility towards all of nature, and so he communicated with natural surroundings that suffered. Habib Malik, now the Head of Islamic Relief in Scotland, travelled with Dr Hany on many field trips when he worked as a fundraiser. He recalls how these field trips schooled him in Dr Hany's language of love, first hand:

'When we'd enter a camp, Dr Hany would sit me down with the displaced and traumatised refugees, and say, "Habib, hold their hand – they're your brothers and sisters. Hold them, feel their suffering, feel their pain. Feel what it's like here – to be hungry, homeless, and hopeless. Be their voice. When you go home take their pain with you and be their ambassador. Speak up for them, it's your duty." These feelings only intensified when we met orphans. Dr Hany was a different person with them. He would be on their level in every way and gel with them – children he had never met in his life. After meeting them, on one occasion he reminded me: "When you see an orphan, that orphan is related to you; forget race, religion, colour, they need you, they need you to help them."

'The language I learnt from Dr Hany went further than talking to children. He is the only man I've ever seen talking to nature: comforting the trees dying in a drought and consoling animals in distress. Again he would say to me "hold them, feel their pain. Put your hand under the sand, and feel the life of the earth – the earth that we are responsible for. What are we doing for this earth, what have we done to it?"'

Habib Malik in Bangladesh with a flood victim

The goat, the donkey and the camel

I was in Mandera, Kenya. Everyone was suffering from the drought and the lack of water and food. Everywhere was dry and sun burnt. I sat down with three victims to talk to them: a goat with a bleeding nose, a donkey staring at me miserably and a camel crying. I tried to comfort them.

Dr Hany speaking his language in Kenya

CHAPTER 8

Global strides

'Truly, God's help is near.' The Qur'an; chapter 2, verse 214

By 1992 Islamic Relief was running projects across the globe which had meant working in two ways: firstly, setting up field offices with permanent staff to carry out long-term projects, and secondly, setting up fundraising offices to publicise crises and raise money to invest in rebuilding victims' lives.

Over the years, the circles Dr Hany drew on maps became real offices called 'Islamic Relief Partners'. These offices were set up in partnership with local organisations to raise funds for humanitarian projects. Dr Hany believed it was necessary to have IR Partners drawing on the support of communities across Europe and, he prayed, eventually the United States of America. He made several visits to each location, meeting with ministers, community leaders, non-governmental organisations (NGOs) until the logistics of registering an office were completed. The knowledge of local groups, the economy, and the social situation meant they could advise and work with Islamic Relief staff in a way that suited the local community.

United Nations recognition

To succeed at an international level, Dr Hany realised they needed recognition from the United Nations (UN), known as 'consultative status'. This would make working with other organisations, and helping a wider range of places, easier. Yet it was anything but easy to gain the recognition.

In 1993, when Islamic Relief was only nine years old, Dr Hany and two senior members of IR flew to the UN in New York. Dr Hany had to prepare a speech and then answer questions from representatives from all over the world. At the time there was suspicion about faith-based charities and their funds. Some charities had to justify their work, funds and projects, proving they were not supporting terrorism, or any illegal groups. Islamic Relief, having been scrutinised and examined on these grounds before, decided to tackle this very subject in their presentation to representatives from all of the member countries. After one week of

scrutiny IR was finally given the special status. Dr Hany and his colleagues returned overjoyed and delighted at the outcome. On the trip home he thanked God for the success and never lost hope that IR could overcome any hurdle to reach more people in need.

Gaining recognition from the UN meant a stronger foundation for future work, and with that in mind, Dr Hany forged forward.

30–40–20 USA

Dr Hany knew there was a balance to strike between spending the contributions they received and finding new sources of donations in wealthier countries. By 1993 the charity's roots were deeply planted in long-term projects to empower people to break out of the chains of poverty. Dr Hany wanted to see Islamic Relief grow into a global tool to combat injustice and poverty and had grander plans. To fulfil them he needed the support of more people, yet at the time they were only raising money in Europe.

The sheer size and diversity of the USA's communities put it on the top of Dr Hany's list for seeking donations, particularly for the humanitarian disaster surfacing in Bosnia with multiethnic armed conflict escalating. If Islamic Relief could start fundraising for it in the USA this could bring them a step closer to setting up fundraising offices there permanently. An impossible task, some suggested. Nobody would take such a small organisation seriously, others cautioned. None of these issues stood in the way for Dr Hany. If he had a dream he pursued it with conviction – the 'how' didn't weigh him down. His next moved proved it.

Laden with an overhead projector, display material about Islamic Relief and Bosnian children's paintings, Dr Hany and a new employee, Imran Madden, set off over the Atlantic. With a Delta pass to allow unlimited flight travel throughout the 50 states, their first destination was the state of Boston. In Boston they met with their hosts, an American aid organisation and delivered their first presentation about their work. The audience were moved by the first-hand accounts about Bosnia and Bosnian children's paintings of their homes up in flames. They supported the fundraising effort, and took home the message of Islamic Relief. A success! After the event, they went back to the hotel, only to find a string of people wanted to speak to Dr Hany about his humanitarian work. While Imran tried to sleep, Dr Hany continued with his twilight talks in the hotel room until dawn. On nights like these, Dr Hany managed with two or three hours sleep. In the morning it was time to leave for their next destination – another city on the long list that he had planned to visit.

Dr Hany and Imran stopped off in each city, often separated by eight or nine hour flights, with just enough time to deliver their presentation. It was an eventful trip that tested their stamina and spirit. It was also a trip with sharp contrasts. Some cities they encountered epitomised the American dream: wealthy, affluent communities with a multi-cultural mix of high achievers. Other towns shocked them, a staggering level of poverty and crime was apparent to the naked eye. In some places they had to tiptoe over bullets lying on the pavement when they got out of the car.

In one deprived town, they presented in a mosque. The best outcome they thought they could hope for would be to raise awareness. The presentation ended and the audience left, filing out quietly without showing any interest or offering any feedback at all. A few dollars were donated, but there was no enthusiasm, no response. Puzzled by the lack of interest from the congregation and tired from their travels they took up the invitation for a meal in the mosque. Just then they heard cars pulling up on the gravel just outside. The audience returned as quietly as they left. Deeply moved by the presentation, they had gone to withdraw money to donate for Bosnian aid. The unexpected was all they could expect on this trip.

Nuts

After visiting numerous states, Philadelphia, on the East Coast, was the next city on Dr Hany's list. There was rarely time to spare before check-in at the airport and it was essential to make each connection. Arriving at the airport just in time, the check-in staff, not impressed by these last minute travellers, asked routinely for their Delta passes. The Delta passes? Where were they? Panic. They threw open their luggage and searched. And searched. Imran checked through all the technical equipment. Dr Hany unzipped every pocket and flap in his suitcase, finally resorting to taking everything out; clothes, folders, toiletries, even his cherished container of peanuts was thrown onto the growing pile on the check-in desk. Finally they found the passes in the back of a document holder! Now, it was time to frantically repack. Imran, the younger and more athletic of the two led the scurry through the long corridor to the boarding gate with Dr Hany close behind him. Moments later Imran realised he couldn't hear Dr Hany behind him. He turned around and saw him standing frozen in the distance:

'My peanut container… I've left it on the counter', offered a perplexed Dr Hany.

'LEAVE – THE – PEANUTS', bellowed Imran, the three words booming on the corridor walls. This time, Dr Hany knew *he* had to listen. With a final sprint they boarded the plane just in time. Though they had lost a treasured peanut container, Imran had found out about Dr Hany's own brand of quirkiness that endeared, amused and occasionally tried the patience of the people around him.

The American marathon ended in Los Angeles, California concluding a grand total of 30 flights, visiting 40 cities in 20 days! This intense activity resulted in another young new employee, Jehangir Malik being sent there the following year, tasked with establishing the first office in the same city they finished their tour in, Los Angeles.

What's in a name..?

Over the years our name 'Islamic Relief' has caused some people to question our connections. This usually reflects their misconceptions and prejudice. Our relationships and work is transparent. If people in the international community claim to be impartial, neutral, and fair, then our name is not the problem; their perception is.

By 1994 a whole decade had passed since Dr Hany had helped found Islamic Relief. It had brought huge changes in the size, work and number of employees. There was now a courageous workforce of employees and hundreds of volunteers that coordinated, supported and managed the projects. Ten years had brought many changes for Dr Hany too. His medical career had progressed, as he had achieved a Medical Doctorate (MD), in 1991. Supporting him throughout was the dedication of his wife who raised their family, now blessed with four children. The very qualities they saw in each other over a decade ago matured into a resilient partnership. They maintained ties with their culture and heritage through annual trips back to Egypt. Sometimes Dr Hany accompanied them, other times he was needed elsewhere, departing soon after they arrived. The demands of a medical career and leading Islamic Relief had come to a point where he knew it was no longer possible to do both: *'I couldn't be a part-time doctor and a part-time humanitarian worker'*. Once again, there was a cross-road approaching. How different the choice was this time. No longer the student deciding whether to distribute leaflets or study for an exam; now he was the managing director of an international humanitarian organisation. Would he lead Islamic Relief into the 21st century or follow his medical career? There was no dilemma; he was now a veteran at following his heart. He left his medical career bringing an era of research and practise to a close. Islamic Relief had eclipsed everything else in Dr Hany's life.

With an office now open in America, consultative status from the United Nations, and Dr Hany committed to Islamic Relief full time, the groundwork was in place to press on with humanitarian work in the Balkans. Work that involved immeasurable dangers.

CHAPTER 9

In the shadows of conflict

'...adhere to justice, for that is closer to awareness of God'. The Qur'an; chapter 5, verse 8

There was a darker side to the humanitarian work that every international aid agency had to deal with; war and conflict. During the early 1990's, the wars in the Balkans, a South-Eastern region of Europe, occupied numerous aid agencies. Islamic Relief was one of them, venturing into this region for the first time in 1992, and prompting Dr Hany's concentrated effort to establish an office to raise funds in America. IR's workers made several trips there, taking supplies for refugees and displaced people in camps. Getting aid to people in the Balkans was a risk that thousands of courageous volunteers braved to help the victims. The more Dr Hany saw of the devastation and violation of human rights, the louder his voice. His ethos always upheld that suffering was indiscriminate. Likewise, relief must be just as indiscriminate; it was for everyone in need, whether in safe or dangerous terrain.

In 1992, the capital of Bosnia Herzegovina, Sarajevo, was peppered by bullet marks. They were everywhere along its carved districts. Friends and enemies sought protection in buildings and flats from the war as it raged above and amongst them, were they to venture out into the streets.

War in the Balkans 1991-1995

The Federal state of Yugoslavia came into existence after the First World War. It was made up of six republics: Bosnia-Herzogovina, Croatia, Macedonia, Montenegro, Serbia, Slovenia and the provinces of Vojvodina and Kosovo. During the 1980s ethnic tensions rose between the republics, until a series of wars began in 1991, also known as the 'Yugoslav Wars' when Croatia and Slovenia declared independence and fought against Serbia. Soon after this war ended in 1992, Bosnia too declared independence, led by its President Alija Izetbegovic, and fighting broke out between Bosnian Muslims and Bosnian Serbs. Three more years of fierce fighting took place, as other ethnic groups, such as the Croats joined the battle for territorial control.

The airport in Sarajevo was cut off so aid agencies had to brave the roads. Islamic Relief workers travelled in trucks, knowing they could be hijacked, with the people inside taken prisoner or even worse killed.

Dr Hany ventured into Bosnia during heavy fighting many times. On one trip to Sarajevo in 1993, he landed in the airport fortunate to catch one of the few flights taking aid workers and journalists into the war zone. When he arrived he had to use the only way into Bosnia with supplies, a tunnel, about 800 metres long. The late President Izetbegovic described it as Bosnia's 'artery, its lifeline that kept [it] alive.' People entering Sarajevo were continually going through the airless, stifling

Sarajevo tunnel

tunnel; approximately one million people passed through it until 1995 when the war ended. The entrance of the tunnel was in a strip of neutral land behind the airport. Even so, humanitarian flights landing there were targeted by gunmen hiding in the surrounding mountains. Using the tunnel, therefore, carried huge risks. The best time to enter the tunnel was during the night, protected by the dark. But this was no guarantee of safety. Dr Hany, unwilling to turn back, took his chance to get across the open area behind the airport. *'I just ran and ran for my life. I could hear gun shots in the distance, but kept going. After you run as fast as you can, you reach the entrance and then have to bend your way through the cramped tunnel for 800 metres till you reach the exit in Bosnian territory'.* The trip was vital for Dr Hany because

Dr Hany meets Bosnian refugees, 1995

it allowed him to assess how relief work was going, organise the distribution of food supplies, and remind the Bosnian people, who felt isolated from the rest of the world, they were not forgotten.

Dr Hany meets President Alija Izetbegovic in Sarajevo, 1993

Part of me...

...is in Bosnia. When I inched my way through the narrow Sarajevo tunnel, I hit my head on the low ceiling – only 1.5 metres high and it bled quite badly. Whenever I go back now, my friends there remind me: "you are part of our soil now".

One photo, one bag and a miracle

Five weeks after war broke out in Bosnia in 1992, Dr Hany went to the Balkans – a trip which he knew would put his life in danger. He visited Split and Zagreb in Croatia and then travelled to Slovenia, both countries, like Bosnia, were rife with ethnic tensions and involved at different stages in the war. In Bosnia, Dr Hany went to Bosanski Brod, a desolate town, heavily affected by the war. Tanks and soldiers walked the smoke-filled streets. Already charred houses were being bombed.

In all of these places Dr Hany met female refugees who all had one thing in common: deep red eyes, tearful and hopeful at the same time. They searched every new face for answers to their simple question, '*where have our husbands, brothers, fathers and sons gone?*'

It was during this two week trip Dr Hany accidently ran into the Grand Sheikh (spiritual leader) of Bosnia, Saleh Jalakovi. It was an incredible, unplanned meeting, as Dr Hany had only seen him in a photograph taken by Islamic Relief staff the previous year.

Aware of the dire needs of the war victims, Dr Hany had planned to recount his first-hand experience to people in England upon his return. He hoped his eye-witness account would help to raise funds for the immediate aid that was desperately needed all over Bosnia. When he recognised the Grand Sheikh, he had an impulsive idea to take him back with him to the UK to recount the reality in Bosnia. With the desperate situation in front of him, the Sheikh agreed and set off for the UK with Dr Hany. Along with them, Dr Hany carried a piece of a chandelier and a prayer mat from a mosque in Bosanski Brod, gifted to him by the local Imam. They stayed with him humbly housed in a carrier bag, on what was to be an epic journey nobody could have foreseen.

Their first stop was Regent's Park Mosque in London. The press had been mobilised and they filled the room. People had gathered to hear the latest about the war in Bosnia from them. Dr Hany pleaded for support to aid the children and to provide people with the bare essentials. His message was reported on TV, radio and in newspapers.

The next stop was Glasgow in Scotland. From there the plan was to travel to their final destination, Qatar where Dr Hany was hopeful that the leaders of the State there would support the Bosnians.

When they reached Doha, the capital of Qatar, they met with a delegation of officials. After they had explained the situation Dr Hany had an impulsive idea. It was a decision that would increase the donations for Bosnia, and force Islamic Relief to take another step forward.

He had decided to send a telegram to the late Crown Prince of Kuwait. The response was astounding: they were invited to Kuwait and subsequently local organisations in Egypt and Bahrain invited them too. All along Dr Hany carried only one second-hand briefcase and one carrier-bag containing the gifts from Bosanski Brod.

> 'We were hosted by the Crown Prince of Kuwait and the Grand Sheikh of Al-Azhar in Egypt. There in Egypt, my home, we were met by the Prime Minister, the deputy Minister, the Health Minister and the Foreign Office. I sold a robe that was given to me in the Emirates to buy two suits before meeting the Princes of Kuwait. In Bahrain we were met by the Prince. I was totally unprepared for this miraculous outcome. I kept the gifts from Bosnia in the bag and presented it to the Crown Prince of Kuwait. I believe this amazing trip to the Middle East was the result of Islamic Relief staff's intentions… they genuinely wanted to get help for Bosnia – and they did. I made one plan, to travel for two weeks, but God made another one for six weeks.'

Carrying flour sacks in Bosnia, 1995

After Dr Hany's successful trip the conflict was far from over and IR's work continued to help the victims of the wars. In 1995 the Srebrenica massacre took place in Bosnia where around 8000 Muslim men were killed. In response to this atrocity, and as the humanitarian crisis intensified, Islamic Relief provided over 700 tonnes of aid.

Shattered lives

In 1999 Dr Hany headed for another war-torn region, the North Caucasus. This area is made up of numerous countries including Chechnya, Ingushetia and Kabaradino Balkaria. It is one of Russia's poorest regions because more than 80 per cent of the people live under the poverty line. This particular trip, Dr Hany's third to the region, was organised after inter-state fighting had left broken families, displaced people and orphaned children throughout the land. He couldn't stand by watching the atrocities unfold he had to see it for himself, and find out what would be the most effective way to help.

It was a short flight for Dr Hany from Egypt, where he was visiting family, to Moscow; four hours wasn't enough time for him to acclimatise from the August heat of Cairo, to the chilliness in Moscow.

Outside a refugee tent in Ingushetia

Chechen War

After the Soviet Union collapsed in 1991, Chechnya – a part of the Russian Federation declared its independence. This led to two wars between Russia and Chechnya from 1994–2000. In the first war of '94, over 100,000 Chechens were killed and many thousands fled over the border to Ingushetia.

After another flight to Nalchik, the capital of Kabaradino Balkaria, Dr Hany started a succession of long car trips traversing the mountainous and hazardous region. Warned of the threat of kidnappings, he crossed the border with trepidation into the town of Grozny in Chechnya. Grozny bore the scars of brutal fighting amongst Chechen nationals and the Russian army between 1994 and 1996. Human Rights organisations estimated that over 30 000 Chechens had died as a result of the fighting. Dr Hany spoke with the Ministries for Health and Education who told him about the help that the civilians needed. Tuberculosis had increased and what made the situation worse was that hospitals had been destroyed and they were not being replaced. Instead, old school buildings were being used to treat the ill and maimed. Furthermore medical supplies were sparse and even water had to be brought to patients from elsewhere, often by their relatives.

That night, Dr Hany made a 'to do' list in his diary. It was ambitious and characterised Dr Hany's desire to remedy the root of the problem.

```
To do:

1 Reconstruction - repair schools.
2 Medicine - to treat TB.
3 Medical emergency - provide ambulances.
4 Cow sponsorship programme - for income-generation.
5 Clothes factory and vocational training.
6 Develop the community training centre - English
  language, computing and vocational courses.
7 The orphanage - provide a budget to set up a
  school/orphanage.
8 We need one office in Chechnya - send the
  appropriate person to run it.
```

The strangest thing I've eaten is...

...shark in Ingushetia (a neighbouring state of Chechnya). Once I was offered dog meat in China but I didn't eat it! One of my favourite foods is the Egyptian 'ful medames' which is a mixture of spiced lentils, I eat it wherever I can.

With Chechen refugees in Ingushetia in 1999

Held up in Kabaradino Balkaria

The neighbouring Russian state of Kabaradino Balkaria was also in a state of turmoil and needed help. It was next on Dr Hany's itinerary. Kabaradino Balkaria is 50 kilometres west of Chechnya. This was a dangerous time to travel, as the Chechen War was underway, with the threat of being ambushed or hijacked a reality for travellers. Poverty was rife, as a result of corruption and continuous unrest that increased unemployment and productivity.

As Dr Hany travelled through the military checkpoints the grave quietness of his companion, an IR country representative, underlined the impending dangers. The early morning drive had started off well and the experienced driver drove quickly. That wasn't to last long. Just when they thought their trip would be smooth they were stopped at the border of North Ossetia and Ingushetia and Dr Hany was asked for his visa. He had one for Moscow, but was unaware that this would not be valid for the other Russian States. The soldiers escorted them to a town a ten-minute drive away, where Dr Hany was held in the police station. For 12 hours he was interrogated, mainly through an interpreter who used an English dictionary to make up his questions. They remained in the military compound, whilst their passports were taken to another police station in a different town. In the courtyard outside, hostile-looking guards paced up and down, clutching their rifles. Finally, just when the rising tension was palpable, the security agent released him with a fine for having the wrong visa!

Dr Hany's trip continued. They were confident the rest of their journey would be smoother. Not so. Within hours they were stopped again. This time it was because of the car they were in: a Lada Neva. This was the

same car model some hijackers had kidnapped a Chechen minister's son in! Anyone travelling in the same vehicle raised suspicions. After explaining who they were they were given permission to continue. Finally they made it to the appointment in Nalchik, the capital of Kabaradino Balkaria – relieved to reach their destination intact and together.

Dr Hany and a volunteer in a warehouse in Zenica, Bosnia and Herzegovina

I was most embarrassed when...

...I was staying with a big family in Ingushetia. There was no bathroom in the house only an 'out house' in the yard. When I wanted to have a bath early one morning, one of the men brought me a tub with hot water and placed it in the kitchen and left. Most reluctantly I had the fastest bath I've ever had. Luckily no one walked in front of the kitchen window where the tub was placed, and nobody in the house woke up. The kitchen had no door.

Chechen woman in Grozny thanks Dr Hany for his visit!

CHAPTER 10

Deeper roots

'Every act of goodness is charity.' The Prophet Muhammad

With the organisation improving the lives of thousands of people Dr Hany's mind buzzed with ideas on how to move forward. At the forefront of his thoughts was a desire to network with the people he'd already met from other humanitarian organisations. This would be so they could strengthen their ties and coordinate their efforts. And essentially help the people in need more effectively.

In the world of aid and relief work, various opportunities to build bridges between organisations surfaced for Dr Hany and he took these opportunities whole-heartedly. In 1999, while at an aid and development conference, Dr Hany was introduced to senior members of another British Charity – CAFOD – the Catholic Agency for Overseas Development. As a faith-based charity, they shared similar principles as Islamic Relief, and they kept in contact with one another.

In years to come, the partnership between IR and CAFOD developed. IR helped CAFOD to work in Latin America, particularly helping the victims of hurricanes in Honduras and Guatemala whilst CAFOD helped IR to work in Afghanistan, Kosovo and Chechnya. In

2006, Dr Hany even went on a trip to the Vatican in Rome organised by the Catholic Agency for Overseas Development. Initially the atmosphere between himself and the Cardinals was a little frosty, unsure about each other. But within an hour the awkwardness and lack of familiarity soon dissolved as Dr Hany hugged everyone he met allowing them to discuss future work in a far friendlier atmosphere!

Joining hands

Another opportunity to work with other aid organisations appeared in Sudan. Sudan was always close to Dr Hany's heart because it was the first place Islamic Relief sent aid to and the first place he, Dr Shabib, and friends set up their first charitable project. At the dawn of

Meeting to discuss the South Sudan peace process

the new millennium, Dr Hany was set to make several visits to this region again with directors of other humanitarian organisations. They planned to meet the Sudanese government and the Sudan People's Liberation Movement (SPLM) to try and bring about peace between them.

Dr Hany greets a governor in Niger

As part of the peace efforts, Dr Hany met Kofi Anan, the United Nations Secretary General at the time, in New York. He explained what he believed would help Sudan: no intervention by the international community, but a joint venture by the UN, African Union and Arab League to work towards a peace process. Meeting people capable of making a change to Sudan's prospects highlighted Dr Hany's growing ability to facilitate solutions to international problems. It meant he could start trying to address the roots of problems rather than reacting to disasters once they had already occurred.

Working for peace in this way was never easy and often involved intense negotiations, but Dr Hany persisted with his efforts, seeing peace and security as a prerequisite of ending poverty.

Recognition and reward

In 2003 Dr Hany's role as a humanitarian champion was made official when he became the president of Islamic Relief Worldwide, which now had offices in Asia, North America, Africa, Europe and the Middle East. In his new role his engagements would often fill every day of the week, and his work often went home with him. There, through Yousreia's management, it was kept orderly. One particular morning, when she handed him the day's mail, she noticed her husband reading a letter with a look of bemusement on his face.

The letter was from Buckingham Palace inviting Dr Hany to an investiture ceremony on 7th July 2004, to be awarded the Order of the British Empire (OBE), from Her Majesty, Queen Elizabeth II. As he read it he felt a raft of emotions; honoured, amused and pensive. The letter stated Dr Hany was chosen to receive the OBE for his service to humanitarian causes. Why wasn't he elated, and ready to accept the invitation to receive this honour? It was because he felt that whatever had been achieved was the collective achievement of Islamic Relief and not him alone. The decision about whether he would accept this award played on his mind for days, until staff at IR encouraged him to accept it – albeit on behalf of Islamic Relief – if that was what he preferred.

Yousreia, on the other hand, could not be convinced to accompany him. In spite of Dr Hany and their family and friends persuading her to go to the ceremony, she declined because she had visited the Palace once before. There was simply no need, in her mind, to see it again. Her curiosity had been satisfied the first time. Instead she made arrangements for their three eldest children to accompany their father. Yousreia had become accustomed to coping for days and weeks without her husband, who would be visiting refugee camps, battlefields and travelling to regions submerged in floods. This was what support meant to her; allowing him the space to serve others, not attending glamorous events and publicity shoots.

In Buckingham Palace at OBE investiture ceremony, 2004

What is an OBE?

OBE stands for Order of the British Empire. An OBE award is awarded for a distinguished regional or country-wide role in any field, in Dr Hany's case it was for humanitarian work. It celebrates an achievement or service to the community for individuals known nationally.

Dr Hany's OBE was followed by several
other awards:

>> **2006 Services to Humanity
   and Medicine Award**
>> **2006 Asian Jewel Lifetime
   Achievement Award**
>> **2007 UK Muslim Power 100
   Lifetime Achievement Award**

*Dr Hany receiving the
Asian Jewel Award, 2006*

Spreading a message

As Dr Hany gained more recognition for his work the opportunity to
affirm his beliefs in speeches became more frequent. Flying in and out of
war zones had a significant effect upon Dr Hany and he would frequently
discuss the issue of peace and justice, which was by no means simple. It
was tied up in politics, history, ethnicity, faith and all these played their
part in creating conflict areas. But the complexity didn't deter Dr Hany as
his goal to reduce poverty, rested on achieving peace. The more Dr Hany
travelled to conflict areas, the more he spoke and campaigned about the
need for peace and justice for the world's poorest people. The crises in
the Balkans, unrest in the Middle East, civil wars in Sudan and Somalia,
all claimed millions of victims, whilst survivors were condemned to live
in misery without dignity, without hope. Dr Hany spoke passionately to
ambassadors, policy makers and Presidents, abandoning formal rhetoric
and political dialogue. Instead, he appealed to their hearts, to their
humanity. Often in speeches to influential people he told stories from the
Qur'an and about the Prophets of Islam and other faithful personalities,
examining the practical lessons the world could draw from them.

At the forefront of Dr Hany's work on conflict resolution and a
key theme of his speeches was his belief in a unified brotherhood of
humanity. The root cause of suffering, he would conclude in speeches,

was down to powerful countries often exploiting less developed countries. He asked leaders of nations to think about how they used their power and resources. In a speech at the World Economic Forum in Jordan, 2005, he said:

> *'There are so many examples and so many challenges which the world has faced, but they all lead me to the one burning question which we should all be asking: had the money which has been spent on vicious wars of conquest been spent on the fight against poverty and hunger, ignorance and underdevelopment; had it been spent on empowering underdeveloped societies and on fighting those other weapons of mass destruction – aids, malaria, cholera, tuberculosis – what picture would we see before us today?*

> *'I believe – and I make no apologies for the seemingly idealistic vision – that we would have seen global harmony, where the strong and the powerful are the first to stand up for the weak and the destitute. I believe that we would today be living in a world in which poverty is so uncommon that its occurrence could lead to the same outpourings of shock and horror as we witnessed after the Asian Tsunami.'*

Back to his roots

The awards, accolades and attention didn't change Dr Hany's desire to be closest to ordinary people, at home and overseas on field trips. On a personal level, he found the awards *good for the public and politicians. For me, I give thanks to God for my faith – that is the centre of everything.'*

Many of the places he travelled to when he started humanitarian work continued to need support 15 years later. Recurrent conflicts kept the wounds of poverty open. What had changed, however, was the way Dr Hany was treated when he travelled abroad. It was a change that caused him to reflect on what was most important to him after he visited Kabaradino Balkaria in 2000:

> 'On my fourth visit to this place I was received by Government officials. I was told to sit in the Foreign Minister's car (a Russian Rolls Royce) for the short journey between the airport and the Presidential Guest house. I was very well received by the Prime Minister, Deputy Prime Minister and President.
>
> 'I remembered my good old days and shed a few tears. During this journey I did not stay in a student flat, eat student food or feel thirsty. Everything was planned for me. I felt … I had become detached from the grassroots. I feel that every day I live I will have more barriers between the grassroots and me. This is the most worrying nightmare for me – to be a VIP; someone who smiles and becomes nothing because he does not feel the pulse of the people or the temperature of their anger and needs. I believe this is the price of celebrity and fame – to be dry and isolated. I wish I never live to see that!'

Dr Hany stayed in touch with his roots, especially in Birmingham which he thought of as the *'womb for Islamic Relief'* because the headquarters of the charity still resided there. It was also home for his wife and five children. Over twenty years after he moved there, and soon after he was awarded the OBE, the city honoured him. In 2007, Birmingham University awarded him an Honorary Doctorate for his humanitarian work. This time, as it was a local, smaller event, Yousreia accompanied Dr Hany to the reception. True to his philosophy in 'Grassroots', Dr Hany used his acceptance speech in the University chambers to thank the real architects of Islamic Relief; the taxi-drivers in the town who donated their hard-earned money, the small shop owners who displayed

IR posters, the youngsters, the volunteers, the staff; he acknowledged them all. In conclusion he said, '*This doctorate is a reward for the effort of the people who are trying to help the poor and needy to alleviate their poverty. It is a reward for the people who suffer. This should not be seen as a personal achievement; I am merely collecting the reward on behalf of these people.*'

Rather than a personal celebration of his achievements, the world stage became the setting for the next chapter in his life, one he entered with even more passion and energy.

Dr Hany awarded the Honorary Doctorate from University of Birmingham, in the company of his wife, Yousreia and their children

CHAPTER 11

Flying the flag of hope

'We ... made you into races and tribes so that you
should recognise one another. In God's eyes, the most
honoured of you are the ones most mindful of Him.'
The Qur'an; chapter 49, verse 18

Along with building bridges between charities and encouraging them to
form partnerships, Dr Hany also wanted to do more to strengthen small
non-governmental organisations (NGO's). This was because he saw them
being forced to close due to pressures to prove their funds were from
legitimate sources. All of this scrutiny was a result of the US-led 'war
on terror', against terrorists globally that started after the September 11
attacks on the Twin Towers in New York in 2001. Dr Hany decided to
hold an ambitious conference in Cairo to address the issue and invited
many heads of states and government officials.

After invitations were sent out, he waited for the replies. The
response came slowly and they changed the course of the next years of
his life and work. Some heads of state had been overwhelmingly positive
and supportive. In particular, former US President Bill Clinton, who was
appointed United Nations Special Envoy to the tsunami, responded to
Dr Hany with encouragement and asked him to set up several meetings

across the world rather than one large conference. Dr Hany took his advice and IR staff began organising 14 conferences, each one in a different country to discuss building bridges, trust and developing partnerships between NGOs internationally. As a result of the discussions, the idea of a permanent forum to build partnerships globally, took root. So between 2005–2006, Dr Hany worked with a host of other charities and organisations, including the British Red Cross, Oxfam and the Charities Commission to generate dialogue and debate. The result was the creation of 'The Humanitarian Forum'.

In 2008, as the president of The Humanitarian Forum, Dr Hany decided to commit himself full-time to its UK office. Although he formally retired as IR's president, the bond between him and the organisation meant he would always be a part of it.

Speaking on behalf of The Humanitarian Forum, Jordan, 2006

The Humanitarian Forum

The role of The Humanitarian Forum (THF) is to create dialogue and strengthen relationships between humanitarian organisations. Sometimes charities and civil society groups in one country may not get help from another country due to prejudice and misconceptions. THF works on improving coordination and communication between governments internationally, and NGOs nationally to ensure relief and development work is carried out in the most efficient way possible.

Dr Hany began extensive travel on behalf of The Humanitarian Forum from 2008, running training sessions and workshops for voluntary and social organisations. Depending on the need of the groups, he trained them in a range of areas, for example how to budget for their organisation, and how to improve networking and communication with other groups in their country. When he met with government officials, the discussions covered topics of trust and understanding between nations.

Within two years of its inception national branches were set up in Yemen and Indonesia, whilst more offices were under registration in Sudan and Kuwait. Apart from these national branches, conferences and workshops were held in many other countries – including Pakistan, Palestine, England, Haiti, Somalia and Libya, – to share information about how they work and how they can improve. Certain places, such as the Balkans, with a long history of ethnic conflict, were in particular need of the THF's workshops.

In 2010 THF organised a conference in Macedonia called 'A HOPE for the Balkans'. But it coincided with a volcanic eruption in Iceland resulting in ash fallouts. Flights were cancelled, airports were in chaos. At the time Dr Hany was holding meetings in Nairobi, Kenya. He managed to get a flight to Istanbul adamant that he must make it to the conference. With the flight crises, people everywhere were cancelling meetings and trips. Not Dr Hany. A friend agreed to drive him and so they made their way from Istanbul, in Turkey, to Macedonia by car; an eleven–hour journey that proved worthwhile, as his blog recorded:

> *The most important aspect of the* 'A HOPE for the Balkans' *conference was the spirit of dynamic discussion between different ethnic and religious groups. Here was Natasha, a Serbian from Belgrade, leading a mixed group of Muslims from Macedonia and Albania. Jason, who represented World Vision, led another group of Bosnian, Macedonian and Kosovan participants.*

'So let the volcano bring ashes – we'll bring the fire of unity. Let the sky be shadowed with dark clouds – we'll bring the light of partnership. When the wind competes with us at breakneck speed, our steady determination will win through. Our 'Balkano' meeting was more dynamic than the Volcano!'

In this vein Dr Hany continued to work for The Humanitarian Forum, relentlessly fighting to ensure that charitable organisations could blossom, so that they could carry on helping people in need.

A living legacy

'To act justly between two people is a charity, to help a man with his mount, lifting him onto it or hoisting up his belongings is a charity, a good word is a charity, every step you take to prayers is a charity'. The Prophet Muhammad

A medical doctor, turned humanitarian ambassador, Dr Hany continues to affect the lives of the world's most disadvantaged people. Whether this is working with scout leaders in Libya, or training civil society groups in Cairo, he is on the ground communicating, building links between organisations, sharing what he's learnt on his humanitarian journey.

But what effect has he had on people around him on his extraordinary journey? What do his fellow travellers say? From academics to students, and volunteers to long-standing employees, their stories show how Dr Hany's personality touched them in countless ways.

Dr Hany at a fair for children with special needs, Benghazi, Libya, 2011

'I've travelled all over the world with Dr Hany and if I've learnt one thing, it's the meaning of the word 'role'. 'What is your role?' he'd ask me in his probing, searching way. He made me think long and hard about why I was here on earth; what was the purpose. As a result, I've dedicated myself to being a humanitarian worker. I found my role.' Habib Malik, Head of Islamic Relief, Scotland.

Whilst he shook hands with Presidents and diplomats, Dr Hany had his other hand firmly placed in the palms of the Muslim youth in the UK. Islamic Relief's Mosley Road office was used for a youth study circle he led on a weekly basis. During these meetings, teenage boys and girls learnt about the meaning of the Qur'an. They debated, discussed and asked questions about their faith. They grew in spiritual understanding of what the Qur'an's message meant to them. Dr Hany made them think. Youth Camp leaders, enjoyed his practical approach and would invite him regularly to their camps. Maysoon, recalled her experience, back in the 1990s, as a teenager when she attended a Young Muslim Camp:

'We were at a winter youth camp in Great Yarmouth. The evenings were pitch black, the wind icy and the ground was covered in snow. I remember that evening when Dr Hany took us away from the hostel to the sea shore. Beside the deep indigo waves that mirrored the moonlight, he asked us to be still and reflect on God's creation. We sat there – our senses alive to the sound, smell, feeling and sight in front of us. After we shared our thoughts, Dr Hany asked us about our purpose in life; what was life about? What did we want to do with our lives? I was going through a difficult patch in my life at that time, but that experience brought clarity and it was a turning-point for me for the better. I saw Dr Hany on many occasions afterwards, and he always remembered each of us individually – although we were young, he made time for us.'

Sharing dreams

The young fundraiser, Jehangir Malik who joined Islamic Relief in 1990, became the UK Director of the charity 17 years later. His progress began on an historic car journey after work one evening.

'My wife and I gave Dr Hany a lift home one night when he asked me, in a fatherly way, to think about going to America to set up Islamic Relief offices. I thought he was joking. I was a new graduate, planning to continue with my law studies, and I had only just got married! America was the place in films on T.V. I never dreamt of working there. But Dr Hany had different dreams. He asked us again, seriously. We thought it over and over, and a week later, we cautiously agreed. We'll give it a go for 6 months and then we're coming back, Dr Hany. "That's wonderful – good! But you know you'll be back after 6 years", Dr Hany predicted. I laughed off his joke.

'We found ourselves in an apartment in Los Angeles, California. While we were there Dr Hany would visit us regularly. As always he insisted on sleeping on the floor, working, writing, contemplating all hours of the night. With his guidance we recruited volunteers, acquired our first office, furnished it and found the means to keep it going. We worked with everyone who was willing; college students and the most humble communities supported us the most. When we hit a road block, no matter how impossible it was to find a solution, Dr Hany would see a way ahead. He has a way of seeing over and beyond things – always keeping focused on the bigger picture. Having set up Islamic Relief's first USA office, we returned to the UK seven years later! His prediction wasn't a joke.'

The end of the twentieth century and the beginning of the twenty-first witnessed more natural disasters and wars. After 26 years of 'serving humanity', there is clearly much left to do. Statistics about children dying from preventable diseases, about illiteracy, about the lack of clean water for much of the world' population paint a bleak picture.

> » An estimated 925 million people in the world are under-nourished (that's approximately 1 in every 7 people in the world) (2010 UN FAO)
> » Over 140 million under-fives are underweight for their age. (UNICEF 2010)
> » An estimated 1345 million poor people in developing countries live on $1.25 a day or less. (World Bank 2008)
> » 36 million people in the world are refugees and displaced. (UNHCR 2008)
> » An average of 24 000 children under the age of five still die every day from preventable causes. (UNICEF 2009)
> » Approximately 100 million children of primary school age have no access to a primary school education. (State of the World's Children, UNICEF 2009)
> » 884 million people in the world do not have access to safe water. This is roughly one in eight of the world's population. (WHO/ UNICEF 2008)

Fruits of labour

The seeds Dr Hany planted between 1980 and 1990 were nurtured by IR staff and volunteers, and grew through the public's donations. The orphan sponsorship programme developed into the 'Al Yateem' project which, by 2010, had sponsored 27 000 orphans in over 22 countries. The whirlwind trip to the United States in 1993, was built upon by a host of IR USA staff. Today, IR USA, known as a 'partner', has four regional offices across the breadth of North America and earned the distinction of being a Four-Star-rated charity, by America's most respected charity evaluator.

In Pakistan, IR's 11 field offices have gone on to affect people's lives beyond quenching their thirst from mountain-top wells. IR Pakistan's programmes include child protection, health and nutrition, and providing education, in addition to emergency relief support.

Though he no longer has to squeeze through the underground tunnel from the airport in Sarajevo, Dr Hany continues to stay close to the people of Bosnia through the IR office in its capital and The Humanitarian Forum's activities in the Balkans. And, in the North Caucasus, where Dr Hany experienced eventful car journeys, there is now a permanent field office in the capital of Chechnya, Grozny.

HRH The Prince of Wales with Dr Hany at Islamic
Relief's 25th anniversary Gala dinner, London 2009

In 2009, Islamic Relief celebrated '25 years of serving humanity' in the company of a long-standing friend and supporter, His Royal Highness The Prince of Wales. His Royal Highness paid tribute to Dr Hany who, *'continues to deploy his unique ability to mobilise people, ensuring that the singular importance of humanitarian work remains high on the agenda of world leaders twenty-five years on … I can only offer my boundless and most heartfelt admiration for all Dr Hany's work.'*

Today, Dr Hany's passion for humanitarian work is channelled through multiple organisations. Often overseas, he travels to where ordinary citizens face danger due to political unrest, such as Libya, Egypt and Yemen; all countries involved in the 2011 Arab Spring of civilian uprising. Whilst abroad he conducts workshops, training small organisations on how to improve their civil work. Dr Hany is there, on the ground talking through their issues and showing them how to empower themselves. In towns not far away from these discussions gunfire is being exchanged, bombs explode and hospitals are in chaos. Amidst turmoil Dr Hany arrives to assess the situation. He is often followed closely by trucks with a familiar logo, packed with medical supplies. Islamic Relief is never far from Dr Hany, nor he from it.

Back at home in England, Dr Hany supports the multiple organisations he has founded and chairs: The International HIV Fund, The Muslim Charities Forum and Zakat House. Between his official meetings, it's quite usual to find Dr Hany attending events of fledgling development organisations such as SELFLESS's 'Celebrating Education' evening, where he motivates young students to aim high and fulfil their goals.

In their home in Birmingham, Yousreia finds contentment in the role she has chosen, in the *way* she has chosen – supporting her family, out of the limelight. She shares her husband's commitment to the world's poorest people; she nurtures the vision with him. Their five children, now young adults, are a source of strength and happiness to both parents. And with this support Dr Hany continues; doing whatever it takes, travelling wherever he must, to do what he believes in. Each day, he continues to be moved by compassion to serve the world's poorest people.

If I could go back in time...

...I'd want to meet three people from the past. The first is the fifth Caliph; Umar ibn Abdul Aziz – a legendary ruler and teacher. The second is my Arabic teacher from primary school, I would apologise to him for all the trouble I gave him. And the third is a cousin who used to tell me historical stories about Cairo and life... he was another great teacher.

Events in the life of Dr Hany El Banna

1950   Dr Hany is born in Cairo, Egypt.

1969 – 76   Attends Al Azhar University and receives
               a Bachelor of Medicine and a Diploma of
               Islamic Studies.

1977–1994   Moves to the UK and becomes a doctor
               with the National Health Service (NHS).

1981   Awarded Hamilton Bailey Prize, Dudley Road (City)
               Hospital, Birmingham.

1983   Marries Yousreia Labib in
               Cairo, Egypt. Travels to
               Sudan to attend a medical
               conference during the time of
               the famine.

1984   Forms committee to help Muslim refugees in Africa. First
               child is born.

1985   The committee found
               'Islamic Relief' with three
               other medical students in
               Birmingham. Dr Hany's first
               field visit to Sudan.

1989   Khartoum flood occurs and Dr
               Hany and Islamic Relief raise £200 000 for the victims of
               the natural disaster.

1990   Iraq invades and annexes Kuwait.

1991   The Gulf War begins in response to Iraq's invasion of Kuwait. Dr Hany travels to Bangladesh to distribute aid in the capital Dhaka. The first field office in Sudan is established.

1992   The Bosnian War starts and Dr Hany makes the first of many trips to Bosnia. He also traverses the UK and the Middle East with the Bosnian Grand Sheikh.

1993   Travels to the USA on the 30–40–20 tour. Visits the United Nations and helps Islamic Relief gain 'Consultative Status'.

1994   Leaves medical profession to work solely for the humanitarian cause.

1995   Srebrenica massacre occurs in Bosnia.

1997–1998   Travels extensively throughout the Far East, the Middle East, Pakistan and India, promoting the message of Islamic Relief.

1999   Visits the North Caucasus and plans out how Islamic Relief can aid the countries being affected by the Chechen wars.

2001   September 11 attack on the Twin Towers of the World Trade Centre.

2003   Dr Hany becomes president of Islamic Relief Worldwide.

2004   Awarded the Order of the British Empire (OBE), London, UK.

2004–2006   Receives numerous awards for his work including the Ibn
             Khaldun Award from The Muslim News for Excellence
             in Promoting Understanding between Global Cultures
             and Faiths, London, UK; the Kashmiri and Pakistani
             Professional Association Award, West Midlands, UK; and
             The Asian Jewel Awards, London, UK.

2006   Founds The Humanitarian Forum.

2007   Honorary Degree of
             'Doctor of the University of
             Birmingham *honoris causa*',
             Birmingham, UK.

2008   Founds Muslim Charities
             Forum with seven other
             Muslim NGOs. Dr El Banna
             retires as president of Islamic Relief Worldwide. Becomes
             the president of The Humanitarian Forum.

2009–2010   Founds Zakat House, a social enterprise organisation.

2010   Travels to Pakistan, Sudan and Saudi Arabia. Awarded
             Lifetime Achievement Award at GPU (Global Peace and
             Unity) event for contribution to Muslim heritage.

2011   Makes several trips on behalf of THF to Egypt, Libya
             andYemen during the Arab Spring. Receives the Friends of
             Pakistan, Ali Jinnah Award.

Acknowledgements

This book was only possible because of God's infinite mercy and blessings for which I am truly grateful.

I would like to thank the following people for their support and contributions: the staff at Islamic Relief: Samira Radman, Fatema Hersi, Jehangir Malik, Habib Malik, Mohammed Afsar and Abdul Malik Griffiths. Thank you Ghada Al-Nasseri for helping to locate Dr Hany all over the world, and Andreea Carman of The Humanitarian Forum. Sincere thanks to Muhammad Imran for lighting the first spark. Imran Madden, Mahmooda Qureshi and Rehanah Sadiq thank you for going back in time to bring readers your anecdotes. To the many other people who shared inspiring memories about Dr Hany's impact on their lives, much gratitude.

I am also grateful for being awarded a K Blundell Trust grant, by The Society of Authors, to support writers producing works that increase social awareness.

Special thanks to Yosef Smyth, the editor, for: holding the reigns of this project and preventing it from galloping off to delightful yet wholly irrelevant destinations; for remaining calm and composed throughout.

This book was made possible because of Dr Hany's commitment, openness and forthright honesty – thank you.

The last word of thanks must go to Asad, for everything.

I hope all who helped with this book, will find the prayer of Prophet Abraham a fitting request:

'Our Lord, accept this from us, You are All Hearing, All Knowing'
(The Qur'an; Chapter 2, Verse 127)

Acknowledgements from Dr Hany El Banna
I would like to give thanks to some of the first volunteers of IR:
Dr Samir Abdul Azim Zahir , Ahmed Almulad, Um Asad Al Shamahi, Hezam Fayed, Mohammed Ali Zayed, Khalid Sheriff , Dr Shamim Qureshi, Rehanah Sadiq, Maqsood Qureshi.

I would like to honour the memory of the following people who served Islamic Relief in the early days, and have since passed away:
Al Faqih Abdul Raqeeb, Mohammed Salem Al Khullaqi, Mohammed Muthana, Dr Mohammed Qutba , Abdulshahid Abdulrafi Al Ashal, Mohammed Azam, Dr Rahman, Akmal Sheriff and Dr Farooq Shahin.

Much gratitude goes to Dr Samir Zahir, Dr Essam Hadid and Dr Mohammed Alfy for their service to Islamic Relief.

Select Bibliography and Sources

Books

» Fisk, Robert. *The Great War for Civilisation* (2005) London, Fourth Estate an imprint of Harper Collins Publishers pp 1020-1026

» Glenny, Misha. *The Balkans, Nationalism, War and The Great Powers* (1999). London, Granta Books

» El Banna, Hany. *Grassroots Work* (1996) Birmingham, Islamic Relief Worldwide

» Izetbegovic, Alija. *Inescapable Questions* (2003) Leicester, Islamic Foundation UK

» Haleem, M.A.S. *The Qur'an* (2005) Oxford, Oxford University Press

Speeches

» El Banna, Hany, 2005, *'Dimensions of Global Intervention'*, at The Meeting of the World Economic Forum, Jordan.

» El Banna, Hany, 2007, at the Berkley Centre for religion, peace and world affairs, George Town University, USA.

Websites

Islamic Relief Worldwide, www.islamic-relief.com

Islamic Relief UK, www.islamic-relief.org.uk

Islamic Relief USA, www.irw.org

Encyclopaedia Britannica, www.britannica.co.uk

The Hadith Library, www.ahadith.co.uk

The Humanitarian Forum, www.humanitarianforum.org

The International HIV Fund, www.internationalhivfund.org

Zakat House, www.zakat-house.com

Muslim Charities Forum, www.muslimcharitiesforum.org.uk

References to sayings of the Prophet Muhammad (Hadiths)

Chapter 1: Tirmidhi

Chapter 3: At-Tabarani

Chapter 6: Bukhari

Chapter 7: Muslim

Chapter 10: Muslim

Epilogue: Bukhari

Glossary

Allah – the Islamic name for God in the Arabic language. Used in preference to the word God, this Arabic term is singular, has no plural, nor is it associated with masculine or feminine characteristics.

Al–Yateem – Arabic for 'the orphan'.

Asylum seeker – a person who has fled their country due to the risk of persecution and seeks protection and refuge in a safe country.

Beneficiary – the one who receives aid from a charity.

CAFOD – Catholic Agency for Overseas Development: a faith-based aid and development organisation.

Caliph – a Muslim civic and religious ruler; successor of the Prophet Muhammad.

CEO – chief executive officer.

Charities Commission – regulates the registered charities in England and Wales.

Displaced person – a person who has been forced to leave their home due to a natural disaster or a war.

Donor – those who donate money or goods to a charity.

Field office – an office established in a country where development projects are being run.

Hajj – annual pilgrimage to Makkah, which each Muslim must undertake at least once in a lifetime if he or she can afford to. A Muslim male who has completed Hajj is called *Hajji* and a female *Hajjah*.

IDP – internally displaced person. Used to describe someone who has had to leave their home due to war or conflict and is homeless.

Islam – peace attained through willing obedience to God's divine guidance.

Islamic Relief partners – global fundraising and awareness creating offices that carry out humanitarian projects.

Jalabiya – a traditional long dress worn by men and women in Africa and the Middle East. It has long sleeves and reaches down to the ankle.

Jumu'ah – the weekly communal prayer for Muslims. It occurs shortly after midday on Fridays.

Ka'ba – a cube-shaped structure in the centre of the grand mosque in Makkah. For Muslims it is believed to be the first house built for the worship of God.

Locum – a person who stands in temporarily for someone else of the same profession, especially a cleric or doctor.

Madrasa – a school or institution for Islamic education.

Makkah – city where the Prophet Muhammad was born, and where the Ka'ba is located.

MD – medical doctorate. It is a doctoral degree for physicians.

Muslim – a person who claims to have accepted Islam by professing that there is no god but the One true God and Muhammad is His last messenger.

NGO – non-governmental organisation. It is a legally constituted organisation that operates independently from the government.

Pathology – a branch of medicine dealing with the causes of disease, looking particularly at changes in the body tissues and organs.

Qur'an – the Divine Book revealed to the Prophet Muhammad in Islam. Recognised by Muslims as Allah's final revelation to humankind.

Refugee – a person who has fled their own country due to a risk to their life, and is granted permission to stay in another country.

Shalwar and kameez – a loose fitting trouser and shirt suit. Traditional dress in the Indian sub-continent.

Shariah – Islamic law derived from teachings in the Qur'an and by the Prophet Muhammad.

Sherwani – a formal, knee-length coat buttoned up to the neck, worn by men in South Asia.

UN – United Nations. The UN was founded in 1945 and is an international organisation made up of 192 member states.

UNICEF – United Nations International Children's Emergency Fund. UNICEF is an organisation protecting the rights of children and young people worldwide.

UNOCHA – United Nations Office for the Coordination of Humanitarian Affairs.

WFP – World Food Programme, an United Nations organisation fighting hunger worldwide.

Zakat – one of the five pillars of Islam, whereby a Muslim must donate at least 2% annually of any excess wealth for those in need.

Index